Special Section on Favourites from Caribbean Islands

Caribbean
COOKING & MENUS
REVISED EDITION

by late Master Chef Leonard 'Sonny' Henry
with Mike and Dawn Henry

LMH PUBLISHING LIMITED

Editor: Tyrone S. Reid
Cover Designer: LeeQuee Design
Text Design and Layout: Sanya Dockery

Jamaica Pegasus Red Peas Soup; Photo courtesy of the Jamaica Pegasus Hotel
Roast Chicken and *Escovitch Fish*; Photo courtesy of Vibes Cuisine

Published by LMH Publishing Limited
Suite 10-11
Sagicor Industrial Complex
7 Norman Road
Kingston C.S.O., Jamaica
Tel.: (876) 938-0005; Fax: (876) 759-8752
Email: lmhbookpublishing@cwjamaica.com
Website: www.lmhpublishing.com

Printed and bound in China   ISBN: 978-976-8202-77-2

NATIONAL LIBRARY OF JAMAICA CATALOGUING-IN-PUBLICATION DATA

Henry, Leonard 'Sonny'
    Caribbean cooking & menus / by the late Master Chef Leonard 'Sonny'
Henry with Mike and Dawn Henry. - Rev. ed.
      p. : ill. ; cm.
   Includes index
   ISBN 978-976-8202-77-2 (pbk)

1. Cookery – Caribbean Area
I. Henry, Mike   II. Henry, Dawn   III. Title

641.59729 – dc 22

This new and revised edition commemorates the life of Master Chef 'Sonny' Henry, whose artistry in the kitchen was recognized by those who visited Saffrons in St. Petersburg, Florida, and before that, the "Old Homestead" Steak House and Mike's Nyamburghers in Jamaica.

With his passing, Sonny's role has been adopted by his sister-in-law Dawn Henry, who adds the modern spice of good down home Jamaican cooking to several of Sonny's timeless recipes.

CONTENTS

Foreword

This cookbook is devoted to people who delight in tasty, spicy food. The special sections on barbecues and menus will be a helpful aid to those who enjoy entertaining. The index also makes the book a useful reference for those interested in serious cuisine.

The recipes in the book reflect to a large extent, the cultural heritage of the people in the Caribbean. Thus, you will find recipes that reflect the Indian, African, European and both North and Latin-American aspects of the region's culinary character. Many of the dishes have been adapted to make use of the food we grow, such as ackee, plantain, coconut, paw-paw, mango, cassava and many others, which are considered exotic in other parts of the world.

For our foreign visitors who wish to prepare at home some of the dishes they may have tasted in restaurants or hotels, this book will be a handy guide. In many cases, they will be able to find the ingredients they need in their local markets or West Indian communities.

For those who live here, may this book encourage a new and happy familiarity with the foods we grow.

The Publishers

Other books in the Creative Cookery series are:
Bahamian Cooking and Menus
Jamaican Cooking and Menus

Some Caribbean Foods

Ackee: This triangular fruit with a red pod shows that it is ripe when the pod splits open. The yellowish edible portion is used in many dishes in Jamaica, where it is the national dish, when cooked with saltfish.

Arrowroot: A plant with starch used to thicken sauces, puddings, etc.

Banana: Used when green and ripe. They can be creamed, mashed and fried. Smaller bananas are more suitable for cooking while the larger ones are more suitable for eating when ripe.

Breadfruit: A green fruit that can be peeled and fried, boiled or roasted in the skin then peeled.

Callaloo: A green leafy vegetable (of the Chinese spinach family) used in soups, stuffings or as a vegetable dish.

Cassava: Root vegetable used as an addition to soups or for breads and cakes. It also makes the famous Jamaican bammy.

Chili Peppers: Of the genus Capsicum. The Scotch bonnet is a variety most commonly used in the Caribbean. Another one commonly used is the jalapeño.

Coconut: Used fresh in the Caribbean but can be had in canned or concentrated form. The dried coconut can be made with coconut milk by processing in the blender with water and liquefied.

Conch: Similar to abalone as its meat is white and tough. It can be eaten raw in salads and cooked in soups, stews and fritters. For the best results, place the uncooked meat on a chopping board and beat with a paddle or heavy object until it is flattened, then cut into small pieces.

Cream: Pour rich, undiluted coconut milk into a bowl and allow to stand for at least four hours (preferably overnight) in a cool place or in a refrigerator until a thick cream rises to the top. Skim off cream and use.

Oil: Pour rich undiluted coconut milk into a saucepan and bring to boil. Reduce the heat and simmer until the water evaporates. Skim off the cream and the oil will remain.

Guava: A pink-fleshed fruit used in the making of beverages, jellies and desserts. When ripe, a guava will give way when pressed with the fingers. Its green/yellow skin is also edible.

Papaya:
(paw paw) Used when ripe and green. When ripe, it is used in condiments, beverages, desserts, candies or eaten plain. When green, it is cooked similar to squash or may be used to make a soup.

Plantain: Member of the banana family. Turns black when ripe and is not palatable when raw. Can be fried, baked or boiled.

Salt fish: Refers to dried salted fish used in Caribbean cooking. Before using, soak the fish in water for several hours or overnight to remove the salt. A quick way to remove salt is to boil in cold water. The soaking/boiling time will depend on the concentration of salt, and tasting the fish may be necessary from time to time. When desalted, drain and flake (as desired) with a fork.

Sour-sop: A spiny, dark, green fruit with a tart taste, used in beverages, ice creams and sherbets.

Sorrel:
(roselle) Tropical plant with bright, fleshy sepals. The sepals are removed and used to make jellies and beverages.

Tamarind: A fruit with brown, acidic pulp. It is used to make candies and beverages. Packaged pulp is available in Caribbean stores.

Yam: Large edible roots can be bland or sweet and cooked in soups or as a dish (mashed or in casserole form), baked or boiled.

Appetizers & Hors D'oeuvres

OYSTERS

The best way to eat fresh oysters is raw. Open and lay on a bed of crushed ice. Dress with lime juice. Brown bread and butter is usually served.

CURRIED CODFISH

½ lb. salt codfish
2 tablespoons minced onion
1 tablespoon curry powder

1 teaspoon lime juice
* flour
* oil

1. Wash fish, and cut into strips. Flour lightly and fry in bubbling oil.
2. Take out the fish. Fry onion in the pan.
3. Sprinkle with curry powder and moisten with lime juice. Allow to simmer, then add slices of fish and heat through. Serve on toast.

EGG PLANT ELEGANTE (GARDEN EGG)

1 peeled egg plant
2 boiled crushed potatoes
* salt, pepper, flour, oil

* chopped garlic (1 clove)
* vinegar and oil

1. Slice garden egg length-wise into fingers.
2. Season with salt and pepper and roll in flour.
3. Drop into deep hot oil and fry until crisp.
4. Combine crushed potatoes, garlic and enough vinegar and oil to make a paste of dipping consistency.
5. Place in a bowl and use fried egg plant fingers as scoops.

GRAPEFRUIT WITH SHRIMP AND SOUR CREAM

½ grapefruit per person
6 shrimps, cooked and cleaned
   per person

1 cup sour cream
1 tablespoon mayonnaise

1. Cut grapefruit in half. Core and remove pulp. Discard seeds.
2. Fill with cooked shrimp, marinated in sour cream and mayonnaise and mixed with grapefruit pulp.

PINEAPPLE APPETIZER

* pieces of fresh pineapple   * chopped cashew nuts
* cream cheese

1. Dip pieces of pineapple in cheese and roll in cashews.
2. Serve on toothpicks.

COCONUT CHIPS

1 dry coconut   salt to taste

1. Remove meat from shell.
2. Cut meat into thin strips and arrange in a shallow pan.
3. Sprinkle with salt and toast in a slow oven. Turn occasionally.

FRIED PLANTAIN CHIPS

1 green plantain   * oil

1. Peel plantain and cut into 1/6" thick slices.
2. Fry in hot oil. Drain on paper towel.
3. Sprinkle with salt to serve.

PORK RIND (SKIN)

* whatever quantity desired   * salt
2-3 tablespoons oil

1. Cut rind (skin) into small pieces and fry until crisp in oil.
2. Sprinkle with salt.

COCO FRITTERS

2 cocos   * chopped escallion, salt pepper
1 tablespoon flour   1 egg
1 teaspoon baking powder   * oil

1. Wash and peel cocos. Grate and mix with other ingredients.
2. Drop by spoonsful into hot oil.
3. When golden brown, remove and drain.

ACKEE WITH CHEESE

3 cups cooked ackees, crushed
2 cups mild grated cheese

1 tablespoon each butter, salt, pepper

Mix all together, heat through and serve on toast.

NASSAU CAKE

4 tomatoes
2 sweet peppers
3 green or black olives

1 tablespoon chopped onion
* oil, salt, pepper
1 French type loaf of bread

1. Make this the day before it is to be served.
2. Chop tomatoes, peppers and olives. Add onion and seasoning. Cut bread in half length-wise.
3. Remove the crumbs and mix them into the tomato mixture, kneading it with a little oil, salt and pepper.
4. Fill the bread halves and press together. Wrap in foil and refrigerate. Cut in slices to serve.

PEPPER SHRIMPS

1 pint of shrimps - in shell
* white vinegar
* sliced hot pepper (remove the seeds)

½ onion sliced
2 cloves garlic
* salt and pimento grains
* water

1. Rinse shrimp.
2. Cover shrimp with salted water and boil until tender.
3. Allow to cool.
4. Mix vinegar, peppers, onions, garlic and pimento grains. Bring to a boil.
5. Pour over shrimps and store in a covered jar for 12 hours before serving. Serves six.

RIO COBRE MUD

1 chopped onion
1 tablespoon butter
1 tin red-pea soup

3 tablespoons grated cheese
* creole sauce to taste
* a drop of hot sauce

1. Fry onion in butter.
2. Add red pea soup and cheese. Stir over a low flame until cheese is melted.
3. Add sauces to taste and serve hot on slices of toast.

SEA URCHIN (Sea Eggs)

3 doz. sea eggs (not the black spiny type)

1. Wash well, open and remove the coral.
2. This can be mixed with a white sauce and served on toast.

Sea eggs are considered a delicacy in many countries. The coral is scraped out and eaten raw with a squeeze of lemon or lime

WATERMELON MARBLES

1 watermelon
¼ pint rum
2 oranges

2 tablespoons sugar
* cherries

1. Cut the melon in half length-wise. Remove the seeds, then with a ball-scoop remove the flesh of the melon. The shell can be kept to be a serving dish if desired.
2. Place the melon balls in a bowl. Mix the rum, orange juice and sugar together and pour over the melon balls. Refrigerate for at least one hour.
3. To serve, place a cocktail stick in each ball and pile up on a bed of cracked ice in the melon shell.

SEASONED BREADFRUIT CHIPS (WITH AVOCADO CREAM CHEESE DIP)

1 breadfruit
* salt
* black pepper

* onion salt
* garlic powder
* oil

1. Peel breadfruit, cut into sections and remove the heart. Cut into slices and place in salted water for half-an-hour or more.
2. Dry the slices and fry in hot fat until golden. Drain on paper towels.
3. Meanwhile, mix the salt and seasonings together and sprinkle over the chips just before serving.

TASTY JERK PORK BITES

1 lb. jerk pork
1 small onion
1 small country pepper

½ teaspoon powdered ginger
2 teaspoons Pickapeppa sauce
2 ozs. rum

1. Cut jerk pork into small pieces and place in blender.
2. Remove seeds from country pepper and place in blender with other ingredients.
3. Blend until smooth. Chill.
4. Serve on small, bite-size crackers.

STAMP AND GO (CODFISH FRITTERS)

¼ lb. salted codfish
* lime juice
¼ lb. flour
* water
1 minced onion
1 diced tomato

¼ teaspoon hot pepper sauce or ¼
   scotch bonnet pepper
1 teaspoon baking powder
1 clove garlic
2 tablespoons oil
1 stalk escallion

1. Wash codfish with lime juice, dry, and mince with onions and tomatoes. Add the flour and hot sauce with a little water to make a batter.
2. Heat oil in a skillet. Drop the mixture by spoonfuls into the skillet and press down so that fritters are quite thin.
3. Fry on both sides until golden brown and crisp. Drain on paper towel and serve warm. Yields 12.

Soups

COCKEREL SOUP

4   lb. cockerel (a young cock)
2   qrts. water
2   sliced carrots

2   sliced potatoes
*   onion, thyme, salt and a hot pepper

1.   Boil the cockerel in water. When tender, strain and skim.
2.   Add vegetables, seasonings, and strips of the meat to the liquid.
3.   Boil until vegetables are tender. Water may be added if it has boiled away.
4.   Remove the hot pepper without breaking it in the cooking liquid.

CONCH SOUP

1   cup of cooked and chopped conch meat
     which has been boiled in 1 qrt. of water
½   lb. diced tomatoes
½   lb. sliced onions

2   tablespoon oil
*   herbs, garlic, salt to taste
*   sherry optional

1.   Heat and fry onions, tomatoes, and seasonings. Add these ingredients to conch meat and liquid.
2.   Cook about 20 minutes.
3.   One teaspoon sherry is often added to this. Only the meat of the young queen conch must be used.

CHO-CHO PUREE

4   cho-chos peeled and diced
1   cup milk

*   butter, herbs, salt, nutmeg to taste

1.   Boil cho-cho until tender. Pour into blender with herbs and milk and blend until smooth.
2.   Reheat to serve with a dab of butter and a pinch of nutmeg.

COCO SOUP

4 cocos	2 slices of bacon
1 lb. soup meat	1 tablespoon butter
2 qrts. water	

1. Chop up cocos and place in a pot with water and soup meat and bacon.
2. Boil until cocos are soft and meat is cooked.
3. Remove meat, put cocos and liquid through a blender or sieve.
4. Season to taste. Add the meat and a dab of margarine. Reheat to serve.

COLD THICK CUCUMBER SOUP

½ cup diced cucumber	1 cup milk
¾ cup diced cooked chicken	2 tablespoons sour cream
1 cup diced and cooked lobster meat	* salt, pepper, parsley
¼ cup chopped onion	

Mix the milk into the sour cream and thin down. Add all other ingredients. Chill for 2 hours before serving.

GOAT HEAD SOUP

1 goat head	12 small dumplings
1 lb. pumpkin	1 chopped onion
1 lb. carrots	* herbs, salt, pepper and a small piece
1 cho-cho	of crushed ginger root.
6 green bananas	3 qrts. water
1 lb. yellow yam	

1. Prepare and clean goat's head. Put to boil in a large soup pot with water. Skim.
2. When meat is tender, remove bones and put flesh back into liquid. Keep boiling.
3. Prepare and add the vegetables, seasoning, peppers and other ingredients. Soup must be of thick consistency.

BEET SOUP

8 large cooked and peeled beets	1 cup shredded cabbage
1 lb. soup meat cut into cubes	* salt, pepper
3 diced tomatoes	* sour cream
2 qrts. water	

1. Combine meat, tomatoes and water in a saucepan. Bring to a boil. Skim and cook for about an hour.
2. Add the cabbage, salt, and pepper. Cook for 30 minutes.
3. Grate the beet roots and add to the soup with salt and pepper.
4. Cook for 15 minutes.
5. Serve very hot, with a spoonful of sour cream and a few pieces of the meat in each soup bowl.

COW HEEL SOUP

1 pair cow heels
6 cups water
1 chopped onion
1 diced cho-cho
1 diced carrot

1 chopped coco
1 hot pepper
2 teaspoons salt
* a squeeze of lime juice
* parsley

1. Wash cow heels in lime juice. Cut up and boil in salted water. Skim frequently. Cook 2-3 hours over low heat.
2. Add vegetables and seasonings. Boil until vegetables are tender. Serve with chopped parsley.

JAMAICAN FISH TEA

3 lbs. of fish cut into pieces
6 cups water
2 chopped onions
2 chopped tomatoes

1 hot pepper
1 teaspoon thyme
* squeeze of lime juice

1. Place all ingredients in a pot with water.
2. Bring to a boil and simmer gently for about an hour.
3. Strain off liquid and serve with chopped parsley.

PUMPKIN SOUP

2 lbs. pumpkin
2 qrts. water
1 lb. soup meat
* a small piece of salted pork

3 pieces chopped escallion
1 chopped coco
* thyme, salt, hot pepper

1. Place meat and salted pork in water and boil until meat is tender.
2. Remove the meats. Add peeled diced pumpkin, seasonings and chopped coco.
3. Boil until vegetables are dissolved.
4. Taste for seasoning. Press through a colander and heat to serve.

GUNGO OR COW PEA SOUP

1 pint of peas (soaked overnight)
2 qrts. water
1 lb. soup meat
½ lb. pig's tail or salted beef
1 sliced coco

* flour (for spinners)
1 chopped onion
* thyme, salt, black pepper, scotch bonnet pepper, escallion,

1. Cut up and soak salted meat in water to remove excess salt.
2. Boil peas with soup meat and pig's tail in water until tender.
3. Remove the meat and put peas through a colander, rub out and discard skin.
4. Place liquid on stove with seasonings and coco.
5. Add more water if necessary. When coco is cooked and dissolved, the soup is ready. Bits of the boiled meat may be added.

PAW PAW (PAPAYA) SOUP (Nigeria)

2 tablespoons butter
1 sliced onion
1 paw paw peeled, seeded and sliced
  - use a fruit which is past the green
  stage but not yet ripe

* a sprig of parsley
* salt, pepper and a dash of nutmeg
3 cups milk
1 tablespoon corn starch
3 cups water

1. Melt butter and fry onions. Add the paw paw, water, parsley, salt and pepper. Cover and boil over a low heat for about one hour, or until paw paw is tender enough to force through a sieve.
2. Return to saucepan and add nutmeg. Mix corn starch into milk until smooth, and add to the paw paw mixture. Stir constantly.
3. Cook for 10 minutes more over low heat, but do not allow to boil.

JAMAICAN PEPPER POT

2 lbs. of chopped callaloo or spinach
2 qrts. water
1 lb. soup meat
2 slices bacon or a pig's tail
1 lb. pre-cooked shrimps

1 doz. okras sliced
1 minced onion
1 diced coco
* salt, pepper, herbs, hot pepper to taste

1. Place meat and bacon in a soup pot with water.
2. Boil until meat is tender. Add callaloo, okras, coco and seasonings.
3. Simmer until soup has thickened. Remove hot pepper and meat (or may be left in if desired). Small flour dumplings (optional) and the shrimps are added. Simmer for an additional 15 minutes.

RED PEA SOUP

1 pint of red peas (soak overnight)
2 qrts. water
1 lb. soup meat
¼ lb. of pig's tail

1 sliced coco
1 minced onion
* salt, thyme, hot pepper to taste

1. Place peas and meats in water. Boil until peas are almost tender. Add coco and seasonings. When peas and coco are cooked, remove the meats.
2. Soup may be served with whole peas, or, put through a colander and discard skins. Small dumplings are usually added to this soup.

SEA WEED SOUP (Irish Moss)

2 cups chicken broth
1 chopped onion
1 beaten egg

1 cup washed sea weed
* salt and pepper

1. Mix chicken broth, onion, sea weed and seasonings.
2. Bring to a boil and simmer for about 20 minutes.
3. Remove the sea weed and add the beaten egg to the broth when it is cool. Reheat to serve, but do not boil.

TRIPE SOUP

4 lbs. tripe
½ cup vinegar
1 pair pig's trotters
2 chopped onions

2 diced potatoes
2 cups diced chochos
* salt and pepper
4 qrts. water

1. Soak tripe and trotters in vinegar with water to cover for 2 hours. Drain and rinse.
2. Place tripe, trotters and 4 qrts. of water into a pot. Bring to a boil and skim.
3. Cook over a low heat for about 3 hours.
4. Strain off the liquid. Cut tripe into small pieces and set aside. Discard trotters.
5. Using about 6 cups of the liquid, add seasonings and vegetables.
6. Cook for about ½ hour. Add the tripe and simmer for a further ten minutes. Season to taste. This is a thick soup.

CLEAR TURTLE SOUP

3 lbs. of turtle meat
3 qrts. of water
3 diced carrots
2 diced onions

salt - thyme - 6 pimento grains
* lime peel - a pinch of sage
* sherry to taste

1. Set all ingredients, except lime peel and sage, to boil for about 3 hours.
2. One hour before straining, add a piece of lime peel, and some sage. Strain through a fine sieve.
3. Add some sherry and pieces of the turtle meat when serving.

VARIATION:

THICK TURTLE SOUP

This is prepared in the same way as Clear Turtle Soup, except that it is thickened with 1 oz. of cornflour mixed with a little liquid for every quart of the soup.

Fish & Shellfish

STUFFED CALAPEEVA (found in Jamaican rivers)

6   calapeeva
1   cup breadcrumbs
*   parsley, salt, pepper to taste
1   dessertspoon butter

2   sliced onions
1   tablespoon rum
1   tablespoon oil

1.   Wash and clean fish with lime juice.
2.   Make a stuffing of breadcrumbs, parsley, salt and pepper, moistened with a little melted butter.
3.   Stuff the fish and place on a bed of sliced onions, which have been slightly sautéed in hot oil. Add 1 tablespoon rum and cover with some breadcrumbs.
4.   Bake in a moderate oven until fish are tender.

BANANA KING-FISH WITH MUSTARD SAUCE

4   king-fish steaks
2   ripe bananas
4   slices Cheddar cheese

*   salt
*   pepper
*   butter

1.   Season the fish steaks with salt and pepper. Fry gently in butter.
2.   Place the steaks in a heat-proof dish.
3.   Cover each steak with slices of ripe banana and top with a slice of cheddar cheese.
4.   Broil until the cheese is melted and the banana heated through. Serve with mustard sauce.

MUSTARD SAUCE

4   tablespoons mayonnaise
4   tablespoons vinegar
4   tablespoons salad oil

1   teaspoon lime juice
3   teaspoons dry mustard
*   salt and pepper to taste

1.   Mix all ingredients until smooth.

CODFISH BALLS

1 lb. codfish
1 lb. fresh pumpkin
1 tablespoon butter, softened
2 eggs

* black pepper
* salt
2 cups fresh breadcrumbs
* oil

1. Soak fish overnight. Discard water and cover with cold water. Bring to a boil and cook until tender. Skin, bone and flake finely.
2. Cook the pumpkin until tender. Mash thoroughly then beat in the softened butter, 2 lightly beaten eggs and pepper. Add salt to taste.
3. The mixture should be firm enough to hold its shape. If not, beat in breadcrumbs as needed.
4. Shape the mixture into balls, dipping each in the breadcrumbs.
5. Fry for about 3 to 4 minutes, turning regularly. When golden brown, drain on paper towels. Serve warm. A tomato sauce goes well with this dish.

BAKED BLACK CRABS

6 black crabs, boiled
1 oz. butter, softened
½ teaspoon black pepper
1 tablespoon chopped onion
1 country pepper, finely chopped

1 teaspoon vinegar
* salt
* breadcrumbs
* butter

1. Clean the crabs and pick out all the meat, including the claws and smaller bones. Save four shells.
2. Mix the crab meat with the butter, onion, pepper, salt and vinegar. The mixture should be moist but not soggy.
3. Wash the shells well and wipe with a little oil. Fill each with the crab mixture, top with the breadcrumbs and dot with butter. Bake in a hot oven until the crumbs are brown.

BAHAMIAN CONCH FRITTERS

1 lb. raw minced conch meat
1 minced onion
4 ozs. flour
1 egg

* salt, pepper
2 tablespoons dry breadcrumbs
* milk and fat as needed

1. Mix conch meat, onion, flour, egg and seasoning together and moisten with a little milk.
2. Shape into flat fritters. Dip in breadcrumbs and fry quickly in hot oil.

CODFISH TWICE LAID

1 lb. saltfish
1 lb. potatoes, boiled & sliced
1 sliced onion

2 tablespoons margarine or butter
* breadcrumbs
* pepper to taste

1. Soak fish overnight. Discard water and cover with cold water. Bring to a boil and cook until tender. Skin, bone and flake.
2. Fry onion lightly and add to the fish. In a casserole dish, place alternate layers of potatoes with fish-onion mixture.
3. Dot layers with butter and cover with breadcrumbs before baking until golden brown in a moderate oven.

ACKEE AND SALTFISH

1 lb. codfish
12-14 ackees
2 ozs. fried bacon

4 ozs. margarine
2 tablespoons margarine or butter
* pepper to taste

1. Soak fish overnight then discard the water. Cover with cold water and boil until tender. Skin, bone and flake, and set aside.
2. Prepare ackees and boil quickly. In a separate pan, melt margarine, stir in onions tomatoes and pepper.
3. Simmer a few minutes, then add the fish and ackees. Heat through to serve.

CRAB FRITTERS

½ lb. cooked crab meat (use local
   black crabs)
2 tablespoons oil
1 tablespoon chopped onion

3 eggs
1 tablespoon minced parsley
* breadcrumbs, salt, pepper to taste

1. Add onion, seasoning and beaten egg to crab meat.
2. Add enough breadcrumbs to bind mixture. Shape into fritters and fry lightly.

ESCOVEITCH OF FISH (GROUPER)

* small fish or slices of king-fish
* oil
1 cup vinegar
2 sliced onions

2 tablespoons water
1 chopped hot pepper
* a pimento leaf and a pinch of salt

1. Fry fish in hot oil and set aside. Mix remaining ingredients together and bring to a boil. Simmer for about 20 minutes.
2. Lay fish in a shallow dish. Cover with hot vinegar sauce and marinate for about 12 hours before serving. (In Mexico, the fish is not cooked; it is marinated and eaten raw.)

FISH KEDGEREE

1 cup cooked rice	1 cup cooked fish, tuna, salmon or
* curry powder	codfish
* mushrooms, optional	* salt
* lime rind	3 hard-boiled eggs

1. Toss together cooked rice and flaked, cooked fish.
2. Add a pinch of curry powder and some chopped mushrooms if available, and a pinch of salt and a sprinkle of lime rind.
3. Pack into a mould and bake for 30 minutes. Serve with chopped hard-boiled eggs.

JAMAICAN FISH PIE

2 cups cooked flaked fish	1 cup cooked, mashed potatoes
1 cup white sauce	1 cup flour
1 cup cooked, peeled shrimps	* pinch of salt
* salt, pepper, chopped parsley	1 beaten egg

1. Mix together fish, white sauce, shrimp, seasonings and parsley and place in a deep pie dish.
2. Mix remaining ingredients to form a dough. Roll out on a floured board and cut to cover pie. Place dough over fish mixture and prick top with a fork.
3. Bake in a moderate oven for about 30 minutes or till crust is brown.

BAKED GRUNTS

6 grunts	3 tablespoons butter
* juice of 2 limes	* avocado slices
* water, hot pepper, salt	

1. Clean grunts, place in a greased dish and add lime juice and water to cover. Add salt and pieces of hot pepper.
2. Cover and bake in a 350°F oven for about 20 minutes. Spread melted butter over them and serve with avocado slices.

KING-FISH IN COCONUT CREAM

2 lbs. fish steaks	* salt, pepper
3 ozs. butter or margarine	* lime slices
1 cup coconut cream	

1. Heat butter and fry steaks until brown on both sides.
2. To make coconut cream, grate a coconut, add water, squeeze and strain out cream, and discard pulp.
3. Add to fish steaks with salt and pepper.
4. Simmer for about 3 minutes. Garnish with lime slices.

KING-FISH FILLETS

4 fillets of king-fish	* a pinch of salt and pepper
1 glass white wine	* a squeeze of lime juice
1 cup cooked and peeled shrimps	2 tablespoons tomato sauce
1 cup white sauce	1 cup breadcrumbs
1 egg	2-3 tablespoons margarine or oil

1. Soak fillets in white wine, salt, pepper, and lime juice for 1 hour. Pat dry. Make 1 cup of white sauce and add the cooked shrimps.
2. When this is cool, spoon some of the mixture onto each fish and roll up.
3. Dip in breadcrumbs, then into beaten egg and again in crumbs. Fry in hot oil. Serve with tomato sauce.

LOBSTER CREOLE

2 lbs. cooked and shredded lobster meat	2 tablespoons rum or sherry
* chopped onions	4 tablespoons oil
* chopped sweet peppers	* salt, pepper, to taste
3 diced tomatoes	

1. Fry onion and peppers until tender. Stir in salt and pepper. Add tomatoes and simmer gently. Add lobster meat with rum or sherry.
2. Continue to simmer gently for about 10 minutes. Serve with plain boiled rice.

MACKEREL ALOHA

1 tin drained mackerel	¼ cup mayonnaise
½ cup diced pineapple	1 tablespoon lime juice
2 tablespoons chopped peanuts	

1. Break up mackerel.
2. Combine with remaining ingredients and toss.
3. Serve in shells or lettuce cups. Sardines can also be served in this manner.

OCTOPUS (called by local fishermen "Sea Puss")

1 small octopus	* salted water to cover
3 tablespoons butter	

1. Cut octopus into small pieces and place in a pot of salted water.
2. Bring to a boil and cook until octopus is tender.
3. Drain, dry and fry in butter. Serve with one of the following sauces.

PIQUANT SAUCE
1 tablespoon oil
2 tablespoons vinegar

½ chopped onion
* pinch salt and pepper

Mix all ingredients together.

CHEESE SAUCE
6 tablespoons flour
6 tablespoons margarine
2 cups milk

1 cup grated cheese
* salt to taste

1. Melt margarine and blend in flour and milk. Stir all the time until thick.
2. Add cheese and salt. Heat until cheese is melted.

SHRIMP WITH PINEAPPLE

24 large shrimp, cleaned, peeled
   and cooked
1 tablespoon cornflour
½ pint pineapple juice
2 tablespoons soya sauce

1 tablespoon honey
1 tablespoon vinegar
¼ teaspoon ginger powder
1 small tin of pineapple chunks

1. Blend cornflour with a little of the pineapple juice.
2. Combine with remaining juice, soya sauce, honey, vinegar and ginger.
3. Cook over a low heat, stirring until thickened.
4. Thread shrimps and pineapple chunks alternately on to skewers and dip into sauce. Grill until slightly golden in colour.

BAKED SPICY SNOOK (the snook can be found in Jamaican rivers)

3 lbs. snook (prepared)
1 tablespoon salt
¼ teaspoon pepper
¼ teaspoon nutmeg

1 tab lespoon onion
½ cup melted butter
¼ cup soya sauce
2 tablespoons lime juice

1. Mix salt, pepper, nutmeg, onion and rub into the fish, inside and outside.
2. Wrap in foil and bake for about 20 minutes in a moderate oven.
3. Whilst fish is baking combine butter, lime juice and soya sauce. At the end of 20 minutes, pour this sauce over the fish.
4. Cover and bake 20 minutes longer.

SOLOMON GUNDY

½ lb. pickled herring
½ lb. pickled shad
⅓ cup vinegar
1 tablespoon oil

1 tablespoon chopped onion
* a few pimento grains
* a few drops of hot pepper sauce

1. Soak the fish for 3 hours in water to cover. Pour off the water and scald the fish with boiling water.
2. Remove the skin, let cool, and shred flesh.
3. Boil vinegar with onion and pimento grains. Add oil and pour over fish.
4. Pack into jars, cover and keep in the refrigerator.

RED STRIPE BATTER FOR FISH

¼ cup corn starch
¼ cup flour
¼ cup beer (Red Stripe)

2 egg whites
¼ cup margarine or oil
* salt to taste

Any type of fish may be used.
1. Mix corn starch and flour and salt. Add beer and beat until smooth.
2. Beat egg whites and fold into batter.
3. Dip slices of fish or whole small fish into this batter and fry in bubbling fat.

Poultry

TANDOORI CHICKEN

1 chicken (3lbs.)	1 tsp. chilli powder
1 tsp. salt	1 tsp. garam massala
½ cup minced onion	a few drops of red food colouring
1" fresh ginger root, minced	salt to taste (1/2 tsp.)
2 cloves garlic, minced	1 cup or 8 oz. natural yogurt
1 tsp. ground coriander seed	1 tbsp. lemon or 1 tsp. lime juice

1. Remove skin from chicken; either keep whole or cut into pieces.
2. Prick flesh with a fork and sprinkle with ½ teaspoon salt.
3. Blend together onion, ginger, garlic, coriander, chilli powder, garam massala, food colouring and salt. Add yogurt and lime juice to make a fairly thick paste.
4. Make a few gashes on the legs and breast of the bird and rub with the paste. Leave to marinate for 4-5 hours or overnight.
5. Place chicken in a greased baking dish and bake at 350°F for 1-1½ hours (25 minutes per lb.)
6. Baste occasionally with the marinade.
7. Serve on a bed of saffron rice with tomato salad.

DRUNK CHICKEN

2 lbs. chicken cut in pieces	1 teaspoon salt
2 qrts. water	* sherry or rum or white wine

1. Heat to boiling 2 qrts. of water, salt and chicken; cover and simmer for about 15 minutes.
2. Place chicken in a bowl or jar and cover completely with liquor.
3. Keep refrigerated for one week. Serve cold.

JERK CHICKEN

3 lbs. chicken, clean and quartered	½ tsp. paprika
1 tsp. salt	4 tbsps. jerk sauce
½ tsp. black pepper	

1. Using a small knife, make two slits in each chicken quarter.
2. Season with salt, pepper, paprika, and jerk sauce. Cover and marinate in the refrigerator for at least 1 hour or even overnight.
3. Preheat oven to 375°F and barbecue to 350°F.
4. Place chicken in a roasting pan and cook in the oven for 30 minutes. Then transfer chicken to the barbecue and grill, turning chicken often, until it is cooked through.

CHICKEN WITH LIME AND OLIVES

2½ lbs. chicken
¼ cup oil
1½ cups minced onions
½ teaspoon powdered ginger

1½ cups water
1 tablespoon lime juice
2 doz. small pitted olives
* salt, pepper

1. Cut chicken into pieces and brown on all sides in oil.
2. Remove chicken and fry onions. Stir in ginger, salt and pepper and simmer for 2 minutes.
3. Add water, lime juice and chicken pieces.
4. Simmer for 30 minutes. Add olives a few minutes before serving.

TROPICAL CHICKEN

4 young coconuts
1 small chicken
2 cups chicken broth
1 cup rice
1 cup chopped pineapple

1 diced onion
½ cup corn kernels
3 tablespoons curry powder
* salt, pepper

1. Slice off top of coconuts and take a thin slice off the bottoms also, so that the coconut will stand upright. Pour off water and reserve.
2. Steam chicken in coconut water. When tender, remove, cool and shred the meat.
3. Steam rice in 2 cups of broth (adding water if needed). Mix in pineapple, onions, corn and curry powder. Correct seasoning.
4. Stuff coconuts with this mixture, placing alternate layers with the shredded chicken. Replace tops on coconut and sit in a shallow pan of water.
5. Bake in a moderate oven for one hour. If water in the pan evaporates, add more.

A DIFFERENT STUFFING FOR ROASTED CHICKEN

1 cup cooked rice
½ cup raisins
¼ cup finely chopped onions

* diced cooked chicken liver
2 ozs. butter
1 egg

1. Mash the chicken livers and mix all ingredients together, working the butter well into mixture.
2. Add the beaten egg last to bind.

CHICKEN KEBABS

½ cup orange juice
¼ cup lemon juice
¼ cup lime juice
1 8oz. can pineapple chunks, drain and save the juice
¼ cup olive oil
½ teaspoon salt
½ teaspoon pepper

1 lemon
1 lime
1 small orange
4 boneless, skinless chicken breasts
½ green pepper
½ red pepper
1 small red onion

1. Combine juices, olive oil, salt and pepper in a bowl and whisk together. Put ½ cup of this marinade to the side.
3. Place chicken in a ziploc bag and add the remaining marinade.
4. Chill for 2 hours and coat the chicken. Cut peppers and onions into 1 inch chunks and slice the mushrooms in half. Remove chicken from the marinade and cut into 1inch pieces. Cut lemon, lime and orange into 1-2 inch pieces.
5. Take 8 skewers and thread them with the fruits, vegetables and chicken.
6. Preheat grill to a medium-high heat.
7. Place kebabs on the grill and baste occasionally with the reserved marinade. Turn kebabs frequently and cook until chicken is done. Approximately 10-20 mins.
8. Note: Feel free to replace the chicken with steak or shrimp.

BRAISED GUINEA HEN

1 prepared guinea hen
* fat
1 lump of butter
1 lb. carrots

1 clove garlic
1 sliced onion
* parsley, thyme, salt, pepper to taste

1. Put butter inside guinea hen and brown in sizzling fat.
2. Clean and slice carrots length-wise and add to pan with garlic, onion and herbs.
3. Cover and cook about an hour depending on the age of the bird. Wine may be added to the sauce.

GUINEA FOWL STEW

1 guinea fowl
4 onions
2 tomatoes
2 hard-boiled eggs
2 cups crushed peanuts

1 cup water
2 cloves garlic
½ teaspoon salt
* oil
* boiled white rice

1. Put peanuts in 1 cup water and boil for 12 minutes until the peanut oil shows on the side of the pot.
2. Cut up guinea fowl and sauté in oil. Add diced tomatoes, onions and garlic.
3. Finally, add all the peanuts and seasoning. Mix well and fry for 5 minutes.
4. Empty into a pot, adding more water if needed, and stew until flesh is tender.
5. When cooked, float halved hard-boiled eggs on the top and serve with boiled white rice.

PIGEONS WITH CABBAGE

2   pigeons
1   small cabbage
1   onion
2   pieces bacon
½   cup water

*   juice of 1 lime
½   cup raisins
*   a pinch of salt
*   sugar and pepper to taste

1.   Cut the birds in half down the backbone. Melt fat from bacon and fry the birds in this. Remove birds.
2.   Slice onion and sauté in the same pan. Add sugar and raisins. Shred cabbage and add to the pan. Stir to coat.
3.   Heat water and lime juice and add to pan with a sprinkle of salt.
4.   Place the pieces of pigeons on top of the cabbage. Cover and simmer for about 1 hour.
5.   Correct seasoning.

PIGEON PIE

3   pigeons cut into pieces
*   salt and pepper
3   tablespoons oil

*   diced ham
2   cups chicken broth

1.   Season pigeons with salt and pepper and fry in oil. Add diced ham and stock. Place in a deep pie dish and cover with crust.
2.   Bake in 350°F oven 30 minutes or till crust is lightly browned.

PIE CRUST

1   cup flour
4   ozs. butter, margarine or shortening

2-3 tablespoons cold water
*   pinch of salt

1.   Sift together flour and salt.
2.   Mix fat into flour by using 2 knives and "cutting" in the fat till it is pea-sized and coated with flour.
3.   Sprinkle water over flour using a minimum amount to moisten mixture. Shape mixture into a mound and roll out.
4.   Cut to fit dish.

PIGEONS WITH PINEAPPLE

½   of a ripe pineapple
4   squabs (young pigeons)
¼   cup butter
¼   cup paté

4   tablespoons brandy or rum if preferred
*   salt, pepper to taste
½   cup pineapple juice

1.   Peel, slice and dice pineapple. Wash and dry squabs. Into each body cavity put 1 tablespoon paté and a piece of pineapple. Close cavity and rub squabs with salt and pepper.
2.   Melt ½ of the butter in a heavy casserole dish and brown the squabs. Do not prick the skins.
3.   Flame with 1 tablespoon brandy or rum (heat, ignite and pour over squabs). Pour in the remaining butter, and roast squabs in 350°F oven uncovered, basting often, for about 45 minutes.
4.   While squabs are roasting, poach slices of pineapple in the rest of liquor for 10 minutes.
5.   Arrange slices on the squabs to serve.

BALDPATE SPATCHCOCK

3 baldpate doves
2 tablespoons melted butter
1 teaspoon salt

1 teaspoon pepper
* juice of a lime
* fat for basting

1. Prepare doves, wash with lime juice and season.
2. Split through the backbone and flatten the birds. Wipe dry.
3. Bake in hot oven, basting frequently for about 15 minutes.
4. Remove from the oven, place under a grill, dribble melted butter over the birds and grill on both sides.

WHITE WING (OR ANY OTHER DOVE) WITH CREAM

4 doves
4 slices bacon
4 tablespoons butter

¼ pint cream (or evaporated milk)
* a few black olives
* salt and pepper to taste

1. Cover the breast of each bird with a slice of bacon and season. Place 1 tablespoon butter inside each.
2. Roast in a hot 400-450°F oven for 30 minutes.
3. Remove birds, drain off surplus fat and add cream to the pan.
4. Simmer slowly and season to taste. Add olives, and pour over the birds.

BRAISED DUCKLING

1 3½ -4 lb. duckling
4 ozs. butter
2 onions
2 carrots
¼ cup brandy or wine

1 cup chicken stock
½ lb. young sliced turnips
2 ozs. butter
* salt, pepper to taste

1. Fry duck on all sides until brown in a casserole dish. Put in the onions and sliced carrots, add browning also.
2. Pour in the liquor and all the stock with salt and pepper. Place in a moderate oven 350°F and baste frequently.
3. When duck is ready, keep it warm.
4. Strain the liquid, remove vegetables and reduce the sauce. Serve with the young turnips which have been cooked while duck was braising.
5. Blanch the turnips first, then sauté in butter.

SALMI OF DUCK

1   duck
2   ozs. butter
1   oz. flour
1   onion, chopped

1½ pints chicken stock (chicken cubes melted in water)
* salt, pepper
* brandy or wine

1. Roast duck, cook till slightly underdone. Cut into neat joints.
2. Melt 1 oz. butter and fry onion. Add stock, simmer for 1 hour and strain.
3. Melt remaining butter, stir in flour and add the stock. Season and simmer 15 minutes.
4. Add the pieces of duck and cook 20 minutes longer. Brandy or wine is usually added to taste.

DUCK AND PINEAPPLE

1   4 lb. duck
1   tin pineapple slices
2   tablespoons oil
1   tablespoon rum

½ cup water
2 tablespoons sugar
* a pinch of salt

1. Clean and roast the duck. Cool, remove bones and slice. Drain pineapple slices and dice.
2. Place duck and pineapple in alternate layers in a casserole dish.
3. Add the pineapple juice mixed with oil soya sauce, rum, water, sugar and salt.
4. Bake in moderate oven for 1 hour. Serve with rice and green salad.

TEAL WITH ORANGE SAUCE

* teal (wild duck)
* salt and pepper

* oil

1. Prepare and season birds.
2. Roast till done in a moderate oven, basting with cooking fats and adding a little oil if necessary.

SAUCE

* juice of 2 oranges
* 2 cloves
1   dessertspoon corn starch

1 tablespoon rum
* orange segments

1. Mix juice with cloves and thicken with corn starch moistened first in some of the juice.
2. Add rum and orange juice to liquid and boil very slowly to thicken in a double boiler. Serve over teal.

Meats

BEEF CURRY WITH GREEN BANANAS

3   peeled green bananas cut in ¼" slices
1½ lbs. stewing beef
3   tablespoons oil
2   tablespoons curry powder
2   onions

1½ tablespoons flour
½ cup tomato ketchup
½ teaspoon salt
½ cup rum

1.   Boil bananas in salted water for 20 minutes. Drain and reserve.
2.   Cut beef into cubes and brown in oil. Transfer to a saucepan.
3.   Add sliced onions. Stir in flour, salt and tomato ketchup and cook for 5 minutes.
4.   Cover with curry powder mixed in some water. Stir and simmer for 1½ hrs. Add rum and green banana slices. Heat through.

BEEF AND MANGO IN BEER

12 ozs. minced beef
1   cup Red Stripe Beer
1   cup water
½ cup mango chutney

*   pinch of salt and onion powder
1   dessertspoon soy sauce
½ cup rice
1   cup green peas

1.   Combine beef, beer, water, chutney, onions, powder, salt and soy sauce in a casserole and bake in oven for 1 hour at 350°F.
2.   Add rice and cook for ½ hour. Just before serving, add the peas.

SALTED BEEF AND BANANA CASSEROLE

½ lb. diced, cooked, salted beef.
2   eggs
1   cup grated cheese

½ cup milk
1   cup diced ripe bananas
*   salt, pepper, marjoram

1.   Beat eggs, stir in cheese, beef, milk, pepper, marjoram and bananas.
2.   Use very little salt if any. Turn into a casserole and bake for about 40 minutes in a 350°F oven.

24

DUMPERPUMPKIN

1 small pumpkin   ½ cup seeded prunes
2 cups prepared sweet and sour beef

1. Wash pumpkin and place in a large pot.
2. Cover with water and bring to a boil.
3. When cooked, but not soft, remove, cut off the top and scoop out seeds and core.
4. Fill with sweet and sour beef mix and prunes. Refit top.
5. Place pumpkin in a baking dish with water and bake for 30-40 minutes in a moderate oven - add more water if necessary.

SWEET AND SOUR BEEF FILLING

2 lbs. steak, cubed
* fat or oil
1 tablespoon sugar
1 cup water
3 tablespoons vinegar

1 teaspoon soya sauce
1 teaspoon tomato ketchup
* pinch of salt and ginger powder
1 dessertspoon corn starch

1. Fry steak in oil and cook through. In a separate pot, bring next six ingredients to a boil and thicken with a little corn starch blended in some water.
2. Pour over the cubed steak. Simmer for about ½ hour.
3. Fill pumpkin cavity and transfer to oven for 30 mins.

RUMP STEAK CASSEROLE

2 lbs. steak
¼ lb. margarine
1 dessertspoon sugar
1 cup beef stock (tin of beef bouillon or consommé)

1 cup vinegar
* salt, pepper, nutmeg and ginger to taste
1 teaspoon marjoram
* chopped tomatoes, optional

1. Cut steaks into cubes and marinate for 2 hours in sugar, vinegar, seasoning and herbs.
2. Melt margarine and brown beef cubes. Moisten with some of the marinade.
3. Place meat in a casserole with 1 cup of beef stock.
4. Cover and bake in a 350°F oven until tender.
5. Skim off fat and add a few chopped tomatoes if desired.

POOR MAN'S FILLET

3 lbs. rib eye steak
2 tablespoons butter

* bread slices

1. Cut the steak allowing one slice per person.
2. Rub with salt, pepper and garlic. Brown steak slices in hot butter. Fry slices of bread in butter.
3. Slip a slice of steak onto each slice of bread and serve with sauce from frying pan.
4. Takes about 3 minutes to prepare.

CURRIED GOAT

2 lbs. goat
1 lb. irish potato
2 tablespoons curry powder
2 sliced onions
2 cups hot water

1 tablespoon lime juice
1 tablespoon butter
2 cloves garlic
1 stalk escallion
* salt, oil

1. Cut meat into bite-size pieces.
2. Season with curry powder, escallion, garlic, pepper and salt and set aside for at least one hour.
3. Remove seasoning from meat and set aside.
4. Brown meat in hot oil.
5. Add 2 cups of hot water and onions.
6. Cook slowly until tender, adding more water, butter, lime juice & curry powder if necessary, stirring to prevent burning.
7. Simmer until cooked (approximately 2 hours.).
8. Serve with plain boiled rice and side dishes of nuts, grated coconut, mango chutney, sliced onions soaked in hot sauce and slices of fried ripe plantain. Serves 4-6.

DEBONED STUFFED LEG OF KID

1 deboned leg of goat kid
1 cup breadcrumbs
* milk

1 egg yolk
* chopped parsley
* salt and pepper

1. Season meat with salt and pepper. Moisten breadcrumbs with milk and press dry.
2. Add egg yolk, chopped parsley, salt and pepper to make a stuffing for meat.
3. Fill, roll, and tie meat and bake for 1½ hours in a 350°F oven. Serve with baby carrots and small boiled onions.

MUTTON STEW (In Jamaica, goat meat is often referred to as mutton)

3 lbs. goat meat
1 teaspoon hot sauce
1 cup chopped onions
* oil, salt, flour
1 cup sliced carrots

1 cup chopped tomatoes
1 cup sliced potatoes
4 cups hot water
* some small flour dumplings

1. Dredge cubed meat with flour and salt and brown in hot oil. Add water and simmer until meat is tender.
2. Add sauce, onions, and vegetables. Cook until vegetables are ready. This process should take about 2 hours.
3. When all is ready, add the dumplings, which will cook very quickly. Add more liquid if necessary.

LIVER WITH SWEET PEPPERS

1 lb. liver sliced thin
4 sweet peppers
1 teaspoon lime juice

1 tablespoon rum
½ cup oil
* salt, pepper, a little flour

1. Prepare sweet peppers by coring and removing seeds.
2. Wash and cut into strips. Season liver with salt, pepper and lime Juice.
3. Dust with flour and sauté quickly in hot oil.
4. Pour the rum over liver. Add the slices of pepper and cook gently for 15-20 minutes.

PORK CHOPS WITH GINGER ALE

4 chops
* fat, salt, pepper

* parsley
* ginger ale

1. Brown chops lightly in fat. Add seasoning.
2. Place in individual squares of foil.
3. Sprinkle liberally with ginger ale. Fold squares tightly.
4. Place in a baking dish and bake in a 350°F oven for about 1½ hours.

MARINATED PORK CHOPS

4 chops
* salt, pepper

* lime juice
* garlic powder

1. Sprinkle the chops with seasonings and lime juice and marinate for 2 hours.
2. Grill the chops and serve with a green salad. Instead of a dressing, pour the juices from the grilling pan.

STEWED OXTAIL

2½ lbs. oxtails, cut into ½" pieces
1 tbsp. salt
1 tbsp. black pepper
½ tsp. paprika
3 tbsps. vegetable oil
3 cloves garlic, chopped
1 large onion, chopped

2 tbsps. fresh thyme, chopped
1½ cups water
2 tbsps. soy sauce
2 tbsps. ketchup
¼ tsp. jerk sauce (optional)
1 14oz can lima beans
10 to 12 spinners (optional)

1. In a large bowl, season oxtail with salt, pepper, and paprika.
2. In a large saucepan over medium heat, brown oxtails in oil for 15 minutes. Add garlic, onion, and thyme and sauté for another 2 minutes.
3. Lower heat, add ½ cup water, cover and let simmer for 45 minutes to 1 hour, stirring often and adding remaining water when needed.
4. Stir in remaining ingredients and cook another 10 minutes.

PORK CHOPS WITH PINEAPPLE

4 chops
1 cup pineapple chunks
8 prunes or 1 cup raisins
1 teaspoon grated lime peel
* sprinkle of sugar and salt
* breadcrumbs

* a lump of butter
2 cups shredded cabbage
* salt
¼ cup vinegar
1 tablespoon water

1. Brown chops and sprinkle with salt.
2. In a casserole dish, place the chops in layers with the pineapple, prunes, peel and sugar.
3. Cover with breadcrumbs and dot with butter. Bake in a slow oven 300°F for 1½ hours.
4. Serve with shredded cabbage, which has been sprinkled with salt and boiled in vinegar and water. When tender, strain and serve hot.

JERKED PORK SNACKS

1 3-4 lb. boned leg of pork
(cut into bite size pieces)
1 cup vinegar
* chopped hot pepper

* chopped onion and garlic
* crushed pimento leaves
* pimento grains, salt

1. Marinate the pieces of pork in the marinade for 4 days, turning frequently. Keep covered in refrigerator.
2. Take out and wipe dry. Cook pork on a grid over burning coals to get a smoky flavour; however, it can also be baked crisp on a baking sheet in the oven.

JERK PORK

4 lbs. boneless pork shoulder roast
3 tbsps. salt
1 tbsp. black pepper
3 tbsps. garlic powder

2 tbsps. onion powder
½ tsp. ground allspice
1 tbsp. soy sauce
½ cup jerk sauce

1. Cut pork shoulder into two pieces.
2. Using a butcher knife, make cuts 1" apart and 1/8 to ¼" deep.
3. This will help the marinade soak into the roast.
4. Place in a shallow pan.
5. In a bowl, combine remaining ingredients.
6. Rub sauce over pork.
7. Cover and refrigerate overnight.
8. Preheat barbecue to 300°F.
9. Slow cook pork until meat is brown and tender, about 45 minutes to 1 hour or until meat thermometer inserted into meat reaches 160°F.
10. To serve, cut pork into 1" cubes.

RABBIT FRICASSEE

1 rabbit cut into pieces
2 tablespoons vinegar
* oil or fat
* salt and pepper
2 sliced onions

2 slices bacon
1 cup chicken broth
2 tablespoons raisins
1 dessertspoon grated chocolate
1 teaspoon sugar

1. Wash rabbit in vinegar. Pat dry and sauté in fat with sliced onions, bacon and seasonings.
2. Add broth and simmer slowly until rabbit is tender.
3. Add the sugar, chocolate and raisins to finish cooking.
4. Do not be afraid of the chocolate, it gives a surprisingly pleasant flavour to this dish.

BRAWN (made also with rabbit, using the whole animal)

1 pig's head
* water, pimento leaves

* few cloves
* lime to taste * salt to taste

1. Scrape and clean the head and wash with lime juice.
2. Cover with water, pimento leaves, salt and cloves. Boil until tender.
3. Cut into chunks, discarding the bones.
4. Add lime juice to the liquid and pour over the brawn in a casserole. Place in the refrigerator to congeal.

ROASTED RABBIT

1 rabbit (skinned and cleaned)	* salt, pepper
* sage	1 cup breadcrumbs
1 tablespoon butter	* bacon drippings
¼ cup milk	

1. Stuff rabbit with bread crumbs mixed with the given ingredients.
2. Sew up cavity.
3. Rub all over with bacon dripping.
4. Roast 1-1½ hrs. in a 350°F oven.

SOUSE (From Barbados)

½ pig's head	¼ pint beef stock
1 pig's tongue	1 sliced onion
2 pig's trotters	* hot peppers to taste
4 limes	* juice from 2 limes
1 tablespoon salt	

1. Scald and scrape meats and wash with lime juice.
2. Tie all meats into a cloth with a sprinkle of salt.
3. Place in a pot and cover with cold water. Boil up and simmer for about 2 hours.
4. Cool in the liquid. Remove meat, skin and slice the tongue.
5. Cut up the trotters and slice the meat from head. Place in a deep casserole dish.
6. Bring remaining ingredients to a boil and pour over meats.
7. Cover and reheat to serve. Can be had hot or chilled.

TRIPE WINDSOR

2 lbs. tripe	1 chopped onion
1 qrt. water	4 chopped tomatoes
2 onions	1 tablespoon brandy
2 carrots	2 ozs. margarine
1 cup stock	* grated nutmeg
* salt, thyme, parsley to taste	* salt and pepper

1. Wash tripe with lime juice and put into a stew pot with the water.
2. Simmer for 2 hours. Add vegetables, herbs and salt and simmer until tripe is tender and the vegetables cooked.
3. Remove tripe from the stock and cut into small pieces.
4. Mix tripe and vegetables with remaining ingredients in a covered casserole.
5. Bake in a moderate oven for 35 minutes.

Vegetables

BEANS IN SOUR CREAM SAUCE

1 lb. green beans (string beans)
2 tablespoons butter

* salt

1. Boil beans uncovered, strain, melt butter, add beans and toss.
2. Season with pepper.
3. Top with this sauce.

SAUCE

1 cup sour cream
¼ cup milk

* a few drops of lime juice,
* a pinch of garlic powder

Mix ingredients together and pour over beans.

BROAD BEAN CUTLETS

1 lb. broad beans (or sugar beans)
1 oz. margarine
2 eggs
1 teaspoon minced onion

1 teaspoon chopped parsley
6 ozs. crushed potatoes
* bread crumbs
* salt and pepper to taste

1. Cook beans in boiling water with salt and onions.
2. Puree by rubbing through a sieve.
3. Add melted margarine, crushed potatoes, seasoning, and enough of the beaten eggs to bind into a paste.
4. Add enough bread crumbs to shape into cutlets and coat with more breadcrumbs. Fry in deep hot fat.
5. Drain and serve warm.

STUFFED BREADFRUIT

1 medium-sized breadfruit
1 tablespoon butter
¼ cup milk.

1 small chopped onion
* a pinch of salt

1. Stuffed breadfruit is first roasted for an hour in the skin. (Roasted over charcoal is of course the best way, but it can be done over a gas burner).
2. When cooked, cut a circle in the top, scoop out heart and discard, then scoop out the flesh.
3. Crush this, cream with milk and butter and season with a little salt and onion. To this may be added minced beef, codfish and ackee, or leftover stew etc.
4. Pack into the cavity, wrap with foil and put into the oven to warm through before serving.

BAKED CABBAGE

3 cups shredded cabbage
2 cups breadcrumbs
1 cup grated cheese
2 eggs

1 teaspoon salt
1 teaspoon prepared mustard
2 cups milk
1/8 teaspoon pepper

1. Cover cabbage with water, bring to a boil and drain.
2. In a shallow 2 qrt. dish, arrange cabbage, breadcrumbs and cheese in layers.
3. Beat eggs with salt, pepper and mustard.
4. Add milk and pour over the cabbage.
5. Let stand for 15 minutes. Bake for 45 minutes in a 350°F oven.

FRUITED CABBAGE

½ lb. shredded cabbage
2 ozs. raisins
2 diced onions

1 cup water
1 cup diced pineapple
* juice of 1 lime

1. Mix cabbage with fruit and onions.
2. Add 1 cup water, lime juice and a pinch of salt.
3. Cook for about 40 minutes or until liquid has evaporated.

CALLALOO BAKE

1 bunch callaloo cooked and diced
1 diced onion
2 slices bacon

2 tablespoons grated cheese
¼ cup crushed potatoes
1 cup breadcrumbs

1. Mix first three ingredients in a casserole dish.
2. Top with breadcrumbs cheese and potatoes.
3. Bake for about 35 minutes in a moderate oven.

FRUITY CALLALOO

1 bunch callaloo, chopped
1 cup grapefruit juice

* salt, pepper

1. Wash and prepare callaloo, add salt and pepper.
2. Put into a pot with grapefruit juice. Cook quickly for 10 minutes.
3. Drain, correct seasoning and serve.

CARROT AMBROSIA

12 carrots
2 tablespoons butter or margarine

2 tablespoons sugar
2 sliced oranges

1. Glaze 12 small carrots by melting the sugar and butter in a pan and turning the carrots, either sliced or whole, in the mixture over a moderate heat till golden brown.
2. Add 2 sliced oranges and reheat to serve.

MINT-GLAZED CARROTS

12 small carrots (pre-cooked)
¼ cup butter

1 teaspoon mint sauce
¼ cup sugar

1. Simmer carrots in the butter.
2. Add mint sauce and sugar.
3. Cook until sugar has melted.

CAULIFLOWER CUSTARD

1 cauliflower
2 eggs

1 cup milk
* salt, nutmeg, garlic powder

1. Boil cauliflower in some salt and water. When cool, break off flowerets and place in a greased dish.
2. Beat 2 eggs with milk and garlic powder. Pour over cauliflower. Sprinkle with nutmeg. Bake until set.

CHO-CHOS BAKED WITH CHEESE

3 cho-chos, boiled and sliced
½ cup grated cheese

* dabs of butter or margarine

1. Place cho-cho slices in a casserole dish in alternate layers with grated cheese and dabs of butter ending with cheese.
2. Bake until cheese has melted and is crisp on top.

FRIED ACKEES

1 dozen ackees (or more)
  salt water

* butter

1. Prepare ackees by discarding seeds and taking out pink skin.
2. Cover in salt water for five minutes. Drain. Fry in hot butter.
3. Drain on paper towels and serve. This recipe can be used for tinned ackees.

ACKEE SOUFFLÉ

1 dozen ackees	1 oz. cheese, grated
3 tablespoons butter	* salt
3 tablespoons flour	* pepper
1 cup milk	1 teaspoon Worcestershire sauce
4 eggs, separated	

1. Prepare ackees by discarding seeds and taking out pink skin. Wash in salt water. Boil quickly and crush.
2. In a heavy saucepan, melt the butter and stir in flour. Cook for one minute then add the milk gradually, stirring steadily. Continue cooking and stirring until the mixture thickens then add the salt, pepper and Worcestershire sauce. Remove from heat and allow to cool a little.
3. Stir in the grated cheese then beat in the egg yolks one by one. Add the crushed ackee and allow the mixture to cool to room temperature.
4. Preheat the oven to 375°F. Butter a 2½ pint soufflé dish or fireproof casserole dish.
5. Beat the egg whites until stiff. Mix one quarter of the whites into the ackee mixture then fold in the rest. Pour into the prepared dish and bake in the middle of the oven for 30 minutes, when the soufflé should be well risen and firm. Serve immediately.

BEETS WITH ORANGE SAUCE

6 beets (about 1½ lbs.)	¼ cup orange juice
2 tablespoons sugar	1 tablespoon lime juice
1 tablespoon corn starch	½ teaspoon grated orange rind
¼ teaspoon salt	1 tablespoon butter

1. Boil beets in salted water until tender.
2. Drain, reserving the water.
3. Peel the beets and dice.
4. Combine sugar, corn starch and salt in the top of a double boiler.
5. Gently stir in ¼ cup of the liquid from the cooked beets and the orange juice.
6. Cook over boiling water until thick and smooth stirring constantly.
7. Remove from the heat. Stir in remaining ingredients.
8. Add the diced beets and mix lightly. Keep over hot water until ready to serve.

STUFFED CHO-CHO OR SQUASH

3 cho-chos or 1 small squash	1 minced onion
9 tablespoons minced beef	* salt, pepper, oil
6 tablespoons breadcrumbs	* grated cheese
1 tablespoon margarine	

1. Cut cho-chos or squash in half and boil until tender but firm.
2. Scrape out the inside and dice, being careful not to break the skin.
3. Sauté onions and minced beef in oil and add diced chocho or squash.
4. Fill shells, top with bread crumbs and a sprinkle of cheese.
5. Bake in 350°F oven until brown on top.

CORN FRITTERS

1 tin corn kernels
1 cup milk
1 tablespoon flour

4 tablespoons margarine or butter *
* pinch of salt

1.   Make a batter of milk, flour and salt.
2.   Fold in whole corn kernels and drop by the spoonful into bubbling butter or margarine.
3.   Fry on both sides.

EGGPLANT (Garden Egg) with CHEESE AND TOMATOES

2 large eggplants
2 sliced onions
2 sliced tomatoes
1 cup grated cheese

1½ cups water
2 tablespoons oil
* salt, pepper and mixed herbs

1.   Peel and slice eggplant. Sprinkle with salt and let stand for 30 minutes. Wash off salt and squeeze dry.
2.   Fry in oil, adding onions and tomatoes. Arrange in layers with cheese in a casserole dish. Add water and seasonings. Bake 45 minutes in a moderate oven.

FOO FOO
(This is a well-known African dumpling, made with starchy foods such as green bananas, plantains and sometimes mixed with cornmeal and seasoned. Here is a recipe from Barbados.)

5 green unpeeled bananas
* salt and pepper to taste

* water as needed

1.   Boil bananas, peel, then pound in a mortar.
2.   When fruit forms a paste, season with salt and pepper.
3.   Mould into balls and reheat in the oven, or drop into boiling water to reheat. Serves 4.

OKRA WITH TOMATOES

12 boiled okras
4 chopped tomatoes
4 tablespoons breadcrumbs
1 oz. butter

1 oz. flour
½ pint milk
* salt, pepper, thyme

1.   Melt butter, stir in flour for 2 minutes. Remove from heat and add the milk gradually. Season and cook over low heat for 5 minutes.
2.   Chop okras, mix with tomatoes and 2 tablespoons of the breadcrumbs. Turn into a baking dish and pour flour-milk mixture over this.
3.   Sprinkle with remaining breadcrumbs and bake for about 15 minutes in a moderate oven.

PEAS & RICE

1	cup red peas (soaked overnight)	1	sprig thyme
2	qrts. hot water	1	grated coconut
1	slice salt pork or beef	1	tablespoon oil
3	cups rice	*	a piece of hot pepper
*	salt		

1. Brown onion with salt pork and seasoning.
2. Meanwhile, add 1 cup hot water to grated coconut and squeeze out cream.
3. Place peas in a pot with 2 quarts water and cook until tender.
4. Add salt pork and seasonings and cook for ten minutes.
5. Add rice and cook over low heat until ready. Add hot water if more liquid is needed.

STUFFED PAWPAW (PAPAYA)

1	green pawpaw (just streaked with yellow)	1	sweet pepper
		1	hot pepper
2	onions	1	tablespoon breadcrumbs
2	cloves garlic	1	egg
2	tomatoes	*	salt
2	slices of ham or bacon		

1. Wash pawpaw. Cut off end and scoop out seeds. Chop onions, garlic, peppers and tomatoes and stew for 20 minutes.
2. Grill bacon and dice. Mix with breadcrumbs, egg and salt. Add to the vegetable stew and pack into pawpaw.
3. Cover with foil and set in a pan with a cup of water to bake in a moderate oven for an hour. Skin should not be eaten.

BAKED SWEET POTATO

	Allow ½ potato per person	3	tablespoons Red Stripe beer
3	baked potatoes in skin	2	ozs. butter
2	tablespoons grated coconut	*	salt, cinnamon

1. Cut potatoes in half, scoop out pulp.
2. Crush with beer and butter.
3. Add coconut and salt. Sprinkle with cinnamon and bake through to heat and serve.

PUMPKIN PUFF

2 cups hot mashed pumpkin
2 tablespoons butter
2 tablespoons minced onion
¼ cup milk

1 egg beaten
2 tablespoons flour
* a tip of baking powder
* salt, pepper

1. Heat oven to 400°F.
2. Combine all ingredients and bake in a casserole dish.
3. Cook for 30 minutes.

YAM CASSEROLE

Yellow yam boiled and sliced
3 hard-boiled eggs
½ cup grated cheese

1 cup white sauce
* salt, pepper

1. Place slices of yam alternately with sliced eggs and cheese in a casserole dish. Sprinkle with salt and pepper.
2. Make a white sauce and moisten yam mixture with 1 cup or more. Bake in a moderate oven till cheese is melted.

Salads

ACKEE SALAD

2   cups boiled ackees
2   chopped, hard-boiled eggs

*   a few strips of cooked chicken

1.   Prepare ackees and boil for 1 minute.
2.   Turn into a colander and run cold water over the ackees, which must be firm.
3.   Mix with chopped hard-boiled eggs and strips of chicken. Season to taste.

AVOCADO AND GRAPEFRUIT SALAD

2   avocados
2   grapefruits
1   dessertspoon oil

1   dessertspoon vinegar
*   salt to taste

1.   Peel and remove seeds from avocados.
2.   Slice in circles. Place in individual plates.
3.   Fill centres with grapefruit segments.
4.   Cover with dressing of oil and vinegar.

BROAD BEAN SALAD

½ lb. broad beans (shelled)
1   lb. potatoes
2   hard-boiled eggs

1   tablespoon diced sour pickles
*   salt, pepper, oil and vinegar

1.   Boil the beans in some salted water.
2.   Boil potatoes.
3.   Mix beans, diced potatoes, chopped eggs and pickles and season to taste. Moisten with oil and vinegar.

THREE-BEAN SALAD

1 cup cooked stringbeans
1 cup cooked red beans or peas
1 cup cooked broad beans
½ cup vinegar

¼ cup oil
½ onion finely chopped
* chopped mint leaves
* a pinch of sugar and salt

Mix beans together and toss with the last five ingredients.

STRINGBEAN SALAD

½ lb. cooked beans
1 dessertspoon oil
1 dessertspoon vinegar

½ chopped onion
* a few peanuts

1. Boil beans in salted water.
2. Drain and dry in a cloth.
3. Serve with oil and vinegar dressing and some chopped peanuts and onions.

BREADFRUIT SALAD

1 breadfruit
2 hard-boiled eggs

* mayonnaise, salt, pepper
* a chopped shallot or small onion

1. Peel, dice, and boil breadfruit till just firm.
2. Combine with eggs, shallot, salt and pepper.
3. Moisten with mayonnaise.

CALLALOO SALAD

1 lb. callaloo or spinach
6 boiled, sliced potatoes
6 thin slices of cheese

½ cup mayonnaise
* squeeze of lime juice

1. Plunge callaloo into boiling water for 3 minutes. Drain and chop.
2. Mix with cold sliced potatoes and thin slices of cheese.
3. Dress with mayonnaise to which is added a squeeze of lime juice.

CARROT AND RAISIN SALAD

6 large carrots
½ cup raisins

* oil and vinegar
* lettuce or cabbage leaves

1. Shred carrots, mix with raisins and sprinkle with oil and vinegar.
2. Serve on leaves.

CHICKEN SALAD

2 lbs. chicken
2 cups diced pineapple
6 hard boiled eggs
1 cup green peas

½ cup mayonnaise
1 dessertspoon minced parsley
* salt

1. Boil chicken, remove the meat and chill.
2. When chilled mix with pineapple, peas, salt and parsley, and toss with mayonnaise.
3. Finally, crumble in the yolks and garnish with egg whites.

CHO-CHO SALAD

3 cho-chos peeled, sliced and boiled
2 sliced onions

* oil and vinegar
* salt and pepper

1. Place cho-chos in a shallow dish.
2. Sprinkle with pepper, salt, oil and vinegar.
3. Cover with sliced onions and some more of the oil and vinegar.

BAHAMIAN CONCH SALAD

12 young queen conch
3 hot peppers
½ cup vinegar
¼ cup oil

2 sliced onions
* salt
* lime juice

1. Cover conch with water and bring to a boil, by which time it should be easy to remove the meat. Wash with lime juice and clean.
2. Dice and mix with chopped hot peppers, vinegar, oil, sliced onions and salt. This is a popular salad in the Bahamas.

CUCUMBER AND SOUR CREAM SALAD

1 cup sour cream
1 teaspoon vinegar
I tablespoon chopped mint

* a pinch of sugar
* sliced cucumbers

1. Mix together sour cream, vinegar, mint and sugar.
2. Pour this over the sliced cucumbers.
3. Marinate for an hour before serving.

JAMAICAN SALAD

1 cup freshly grated coconut
2 cups finely shredded cabbage
1 cup pineapple cubes

1 cup mayonnaise
* lettuce leaves

1. Combine coconut, cabbage and pineapple with mayonnaise, mixing well.
2. Chill and serve on lettuce leaves.

LOBSTER SALAD

1 cup mayonnaise
1 teaspoon onion powder
* lobster meat
* dressing

1 dessertspoon creole sauce
* shredded lettuce
* a few drops of lime juice

1. For each person arrange shredded lettuce on a plate.
2. Top with a helping of meat which has been tossed with the dressing.
3. Garnish with olives and strips of celery.

ONION SALAD

12 small onions
2 chopped tomatoes
* a handful of currants or raisins

* salt
* parsley
* oil and vinegar to taste

1. Peel and boil onions in a small amount of salted water.
2. When cooked, add tomatoes, oil, vinegar, parsley and currants. Serve cold.

SWEET PEPPER SALAD

2 red sweet peppers
2 green sweet peppers

2 tablespoons oil
* oil and vinegar to taste

1. Cut and slice peppers.
2. Take out veins and seeds.
3. Sauté quickly in oil.
4. Drain. Add oil and vinegar with a pinch of salt.

POTATO SALAD

(A golden rule is that this must be made while the potatoes are still hot.)

6   boiled and diced potatoes
½   diced onion
1   tablespoon flour
1   tablespoon vinegar
1   teaspoon sugar

1   tablespoon chopped parsley
6   boiled and sliced frankfurters
    (or vienna sausage)
2   tablespoons oil
*   salt, pepper

1.   Fry frankfurters, with onion in some oil.
2.   Add 1 tablespoon flour and blend.
3.   Add sugar, vinegar, parsley, salt and pepper.
4.   Mix together well and pour over the potatoes. Toss lightly.

PUMPKIN SALAD

½   pumpkin, peeled and boiled
1   teaspoon mixed herbs
1   tablespoon oil

1   dessertspoon vinegar
*   a few lettuce leaves

1.   Place slices of firm boiled pumpkin on lettuce leaves.
2.   Make a dressing of herbs and oil and pour over pumpkin.

RICE OR MACARONI SALAD

2   cups cold cooked rice or macaroni
2   ozs. lean ham
4   stalks escallion
1   tomato
4   slices cucumber

*   herbs
2   red sweet peppers
2   green sweet peppers
2   tablespoons oil
*   oil and vinegar to taste

1.   Mix diced vegetables and rice with herbs and ham.
2.   Pour dressing over salad.

DRESSING

1   dessertspoon oil
1   dessertspoon vinegar

1   teaspoon soya sauce

Mix well together.

SHRIMP SALAD WITH COCONUT CREAM

1 cup milk	2 chopped sweet peppers
1 cup grated coconut	2 tablespoons soya sauce
1 tablespoon oil	1 tablespoon chopped peanuts
1 teaspoon salt	2 lbs. shrimp (cooked and peeled)
2 minced shallots	

1. Combine milk and coconut in saucepan and bring to boil. Remove from heat and soak for 30 minutes.
2. Press through a sieve to extract cream. Discard pulp.
3. Heat oil, and fry the shallots and peppers.
4. Remove from heat. Add soya sauce and peanuts. Combine with coconut cream.
5. Arrange shrimps on a dish and pour dressing over them. Reserve a few shrimps for garnish and chill slightly to serve.

SALAD CREOLE

$2/3$ pineapple	* pinch of salt
$1/3$ of a tomato per person	* squeeze of lime juice
½ cup fresh cream	* chopped onion
1 tablespoon ketchup	

1. Cut pineapple into thin strips and dice tomato.
2. Combine next 4 ingredients and pour over salad.
3. Serve on lettuce leaves and top with a sprinkle of chopped onions.

TROPICAL SALAD

1 cup grated coconut	1 cup seeded tangerine segments
1 cup diced pineapple	1 cup mayonnaise

Combine ingredients and serve on cabbage leaves or lettuce leaves.

Dressings & Sauces

COOKED SALAD DRESSING

2 ozs. butter
1 beaten egg
½ cup milk
¼ cup sugar

1 teaspoon dry mustard
½ cup vinegar
* pinch of salt

1. Melt butter. Add egg and milk and stir in sugar, salt and mustard, which have been blended with some vinegar.
2. Gradually add the rest of vinegar. Stir over low heat in a double boiler until thickened. Do not allow to boil.
3. Cool and refrigerate.

HONEY DRESSING FOR FRUIT SALADS

½ cup vinegar
2 tablespoons honey

½ cup lime juice
3 tablespoons crushed pineapple

Mix together and chill.

A BASIC WHITE SAUCE

1 tablespoon margarine
½ cup flour

1 cup milk
* salt

1. Melt 2 tablespoons margarine on low heat.
2. Add ½ cup flour slowly, while stirring with 1 cup of milk, and a pinch of salt until mixture thickens.
3. Do not allow to burn.

A HOT DRESSING

½ cup peanut butter
¼ cup tomato ketchup

¼ cup milk
* a few drops hot sauce

1. Mix to a paste, adding more milk if needed.
2. Use over onions, cucumbers or sweet peppers.

OIL AND VINEGAR

¼ cup oil
¹⁄₆ cup vinegar

1 dessertspoon dry mustard
* pinch of salt

Mix well together.

SONNY'S SALAD DRESSING

¼ cup vinegar
2 teaspoons sugar

1 teaspoon mint jelly
* a squeeze of lime and a pinch of salt

Blend together and chill.

A DRESSING FOR SEA FOOD

4 tablespoons mayonnaise
4 tablespoons french dressing
2 tablespoons mango chutney

1 teaspoon lime juice
* a pinch of curry powder
* salt and pepper to taste

Combine and mix all ingredients.

SPICY DRESSING

3 tablespoons vinegar
2 tablespoons sugar

1 tablespoon powdered ginger

Blend together and chill. Delicious on crisp green salad.

TWO-MINUTE MAYONNAISE

1 teaspoon sugar
½ teaspoon salt
¼ teaspoon dry mustard

½ cup evaporated milk
½ cup oil
2 tablespoons vinegar

1. Mix all ingredients, except oil and vinegar.
2. Add oil gradually in a thin stream and beat well.
3. Finally, add vinegar slowly, continuing to beat till smooth.

DEVIL'S SAUCE

2 tablespoons brown sugar
1 dessertspoon creole sauce
3 tablespoons ketchup
¼ teaspoon hot sauce

1 tablespoon guava jelly
¼ teaspoon salt
3 tablespoons vinegar

1. Mix all ingredients together in a saucepan and simmer for 2 minutes.
2. Cool and chill.

EGG SAUCE

½ pint evaporated milk
2 eggs
1 teaspoon vinegar

1 teaspoon lime juice
½ teaspoon pepper and salt

1. Hard boil eggs and chop.
2. Mix with milk and other ingredients. Excellent over salads.

HOT PEPPER SAUCE

4 hot peppers
1 teaspoon oil
1 teaspoon creole sauce

1 teaspoon ketchup
1 teaspoon vinegar
* salt to taste

1. Put peppers, and other ingredients through a blender or mincer.
2. Bottle. Makes 1 bottle.

MARINA SAUCE

¼ cup oil
1 clove crushed garlic
2 teaspoons minced parsley

3 cups diced tomatoes
1 chopped sweet pepper
* salt to taste

Mix well together and simmer slowly for 30 minutes. Cool and chill.

MARMALADE SAUCE

6 teaspoons dry mustard
* marmalade to taste

2 teaspoons rum
* soya sauce

1. Mix mustard with some rum to make a paste.
2. Add marmalade and a few drops of soya sauce.
3. Serve with barbecued dishes.

PEANUT SAUCE

2 cups crushed peanuts
1 tablespoon chopped onion
3 tomatoes
1 tablespoon fat

3 cups water
2 teaspoons curry powder
* salt

1. Put nuts into salted water and boil for 15 minutes.
2. Fry onions and tomatoes and add to peanut mixture with curry powder.
3. Simmer for about 20 minutes, stirring frequently.

PEPPERMINT SAUCE

2 egg whites
2 cups thin cream (evaporated milk)

1 tablespoon sugar
2 tablespoons crème de menthe

1. Beat egg whites stiff.
2. Fold in cream, sugar and crème de menthe. Goes well with a fruit salad.

RUM SAUCE

4 ozs. butter
2 ozs. granulated sugar

2 tablespoons rum

1. Cream butter and sugar and add rum very slowly.
2. Beat well and keep cool.

SABAYON SAUCE

4 ozs. sugar
2 tablespoons sherry

3 egg yolks
* few drops vanilla

1. Cream sugar and yolks together over a gentle heat.
2. Add vanilla. Gradually add sherry and whisk vigorously until frothy and firm.
3. Use immediately.

SWEET AND SOUR SAUCE

6 chopped shallots
2 tablespoons vinegar
1½ tablespoons brown sugar
½ teaspoon ketchup

1½ cups pineapple juice
1 teaspoon soya sauce
½ cup water
3 teaspoons cornstarch

1. Mix all ingredients except water and corn starch and simmer gently for about 40 minutes.
2. Mix corn starch with water and add to the sauce.
3. Simmer for 5 minutes more, stirring until sauce thickens.

Barbecues

BARBECUE COOKING CHART

RARE	4 - 5 lbs.	Roast 2 - 2½ hrs.
MEDIUM	4 - 5 lbs.	Roast 2½ - 3 hrs.
WELL DONE	4 - 5 lbs.	Roast 3 - 4 hrs.

BACON-WRAPPED FRANKFURTERS

8 rashers bacon
4 teaspoons mustard

1 lb. frankfurters
4 ozs. cheddar cheese, sliced

1. Barbecue the frankfurters over medium coals for about 15 minutes, then slice them lengthways, almost through. Fill with cheese slices and press the frankfurters together again.
2. Spread the rashers of bacon with mustard and wrap around the frankfurters, securing the ends with wooden cocktail sticks.
3. Place on the grill again and cook over medium coals for a further 5 minutes, or until cheese melts and bacon is crisp.
4. Serve with a mixed green salad and potato chips. Serves 4.

BAKED RED SNAPPER IN SAVOURY BARBECUE SAUCE

1 3 lb. red snapper
6 tablespoons butter
½ cup chopped onions
2 cups chopped celery
¼ cup chopped green peppers
3 cups canned tomatoes
1 tablespoon Worcestershire /
   Pickapeppa sauce

1 tablespoon ketchup
1 teaspoon chili powder
½ lemon, finely sliced
1 teaspoon salt
2 bay leaves
2 teaspoons sugar
1 red pepper

1. Preheat oven to 350°F. Dredge snapper inside and out with seasoned flour baking pan.
2. In a pot, melt butter. Add onions, celery and green peppers.
3. Simmer until celery is tender. Add other remaining ingredients and simmer for 15 minutes.
4. Pour sauce over the fish. Bake approximately 45 minutes, basting frequently. Serves 4-5 people.

BARBECUED CHICKEN

1   2 ½ lb. chicken, cut in serving pieces
*   black pepper

*   salt to taste
*   garlic

SAUCE
¼ cup chopped onions
½ cup water
2 tablespoons vinegar
1 tablespoon Worcestershire/
  Pickapeppa sauce
¼ cup lemon juice
2 tablespoons sugar
1 cup chili/tomato sauce

¼ teaspoon paprika
½ teaspoon salt
1 teaspoon black pepper
1 teaspoon prepared mustard
1 teaspoon ketchup
1 tablespoon butter
*   hot pepper sauce to taste

1.   Season chicken liberally with salt, black pepper, garlic. Let stand 1 hour.
2.   To prepare sauce: Sauté onions till brown. Add other sauce ingredients and simmer for 15 minutes, then cool. Broil chicken.
3.   Add sauce when chicken is nearly done (after about 1 hour), basting continually. Serves 4.

BARBECUED CHICKEN WINGS

2 lbs. chicken wings
3 tablespoons honey
3 tablespoons vinegar
2 tablespoons sugar
3 tablespoons soy sauce

1 large clove garlic, crushed
1 stock cube
¼ pint hot water
1 tablespoon sherry

1.   Cut and trim chicken wings. Place in a bowl.
2.   Blend together honey, vinegar, sugar, soy sauce and garlic, and pour over the meat.
3.   Dissolve stock cube in the hot water, then add the sherry. Add to the other ingredients in the bowl and stir together.
4.   Leave to marinate for 8 to 12 hours or overnight in the refrigerator. Preheat the oven to moderately slow at 335°F.
5.   Arrange chicken wings on a rack in a roast pan and baste well with the marinade.
6.   Bake, uncovered, until golden brown, basting occasionally with the sauce, turning once during the cooking time. If served as a party-time snack, eat with fingers and provide a finger bowl of warm water and serviettes to wipe fingers.

BARBECUED CHICKEN WITH SPECIAL SAUCE

1 3 lb. chicken
1 cup tomato sauce or ketchup
1 teaspoon creole sauce
2 tablespoons vinegar

1 teaspoon dry mustard
1 teaspoon sugar
*   a drop or two of hot sauce

1.   Cut chicken into pieces.
2.   Season with salt and pepper and grill over hot coals, basting frequently with sauce made by combining last 6 ingredients and bring to a boil.

BARBECUED LAMB CHOPS

4 lbs. lamb chops
1 teaspoon prepared mustard
1 piece ginger, beaten
2 medium-sized onions, sliced
1 tablespoon salad oil
1 cup water
* salt to taste

2 tablespoons chili/tomato sauce
1 tablespoon Worcestershire/
  Pickapeppa sauce
1 tablespoon vinegar
* hot pepper sauce to taste
* black pepper

1. Season chops with mustard, ginger, salt and pepper. Place sliced onions over chops in baking pan.
2. Combine other ingredients and pour over onions and chops. Bake, covered, in moderate oven, basting frequently, for approximately 15-20 minutes or until done. Remove lid 10 minutes before chops are cooked. Serves 6.

BARBECUED MEATBALLS

1 lb. ground beef
2 tablespoons chopped parsley
1 tablespoon bread crumbs
1 teaspoon salt
½ large onion
1 sprig thyme, chopped

1 egg yolk
1 tablespoon soft butter
1 teaspoon lemon juice
1 teaspoon black pepper
1 small sweet pepper
2 whole pimento grains

SAUCE
1 large sweet pepper
1 clove garlic
1 cup ketchup
1 teaspoon vinegar
1 piece ginger

1 large onion
1 carrot (cut up in long strips)
2 tablespoons sugar
½ teaspoon salt (to taste)

1. To prepare sauce: sauté sweet pepper, onion, garlic, carrot in butter.
2. Add other ingredients, then simmer for 20 minutes.
3. Meanwhile, combine meatball ingredients, mould into balls.
4. Skewer balls and place over flame, turning and basting continually with sauce. Serves 4.

BARBECUED ORIENTAL CHICKEN

1 cup soy sauce
1 cup sake (Japanese rice wine) or
  1 cup grapefruit juice or 1 cup dry sherry
¼ cup cooking oil

1 teaspoon sugar
½ teaspoon grated fresh ginger root or
  ground ginger
* one 2½ pound chicken, cut up

1. Mix together soy sauce, sake or grapefruit juice or sherry, sugar and ginger in a large shallow dish. Add chicken, turning to coat both sides.
2. Cover and marinate in refrigerator, several hours or overnight, turning occasionally. Remove chicken from marinade and brush with oil.
3. Grill about 6 inches from source of heat, brushing with marinade and turning frequently until brown and tender. Serves 4.

BARBECUED PERCH

5 lbs. perch	1 tablespoon Worcestershire/Pickapeppa
1 cup celery	sauce
1 cup onions	2 tablespoons vinegar
1 cup ketchup	2 tablespoons sugar
1 tablespoon prepared mustard	

1. Grill fish for 10 minutes. Meanwhile, sauté celery and onions.
2. Combine other ingredients, bring to a boil. Baste fish with sauce, cooking for another 10 minutes. Serves 6-8.

BARBECUED SPARE RIBS (BAKED)
(Use the American-style pork spare ribs for this succulent recipe. If you can do the ribs over a good bed of charcoal, attending carefully to the basting, so much the better!)

5 to 6 lbs. spare ribs cut in serving pieces	2 tablespoons lemon juice
1 lemon thinly sliced	1 teaspoon chili powder
¼ cup molasses	1 tablespoon celery seed
¼ cup prepared mustard	2 tablespoons Pickapeppa sauce
2 tablespoons vinegar	½ cup tomato ketchup
* salt to taste	

1. Place spare ribs, meat side up, in a shallow pan. Sprinkle with salt. Top with lemon slices. Bake in a moderate oven 350°F for 30 minutes.
2. Combine remaining ingredients and blend well. Remove lemon slices. Brush spareribs with mixture; turn and continue baking one hour longer, basting frequently. Serve hot.

BARBECUED SPARE RIBS

2 lbs. spare ribs, cut in serving pieces	¼ oz. garlic powder
2 teaspoons salt	¼ oz. onion powder
4 pimento grains, crushed	½ cup paprika
* oregano	¼ cup lemon juice

Sauce

¼ cup chopped onions	2 tablespoons brown sugar
1 tablespoon fat	½ cup chili/tomato sauce
½ cup water	½ teaspoon paprika
2 tablespoons vinegar	1 teaspoon black pepper
1 tablespoon Worcestershire/	1 teaspoon prepared mustard
Pickapeppa sauce	* hot pepper sauce to taste

1. Season ribs with mixture of salt, oregano, garlic, onion and paprika. Rub into meat well.
2. Place ribs in moderate oven with a small amount of water, and cover. Cook for approximately ½ hour until almost tender. Remove from oven and cool.
3. Place ribs on rack over coals, and turn continually until done (approximately 10 minutes).
4. Make sauce by combining all ingredients and simmering for 10 minutes. Just a few minutes removing from rack, brush ribs with sauce.

BARBECUED STANDING RIBS (BEEF)

8 to 10 lbs. ribs
*   salt

*   black pepper
*   garlic powder

SAUCE
14 ozs. ketchup
½ cup white vinegar
1 teaspoon sugar
⅛ teaspoon salt
½ teaspoon cumin

1 teaspoon coriander
⅛ teaspoon paprika
⅛ teaspoon saffron
¼ teaspoon ground ginger
1 red pepper, finely chopped

1. Season ribs liberally with salt, pepper, garlic powder; let stand overnight. When ready to cook, skewer beef, and cook over coals, turning very slowly, for about 2-3 hours.
2. Meanwhile, combine sauce ingredients, simmer for 15 minutes. Baste ribs with sauce only 15 minutes before removing from coals. Serves 15 people.
3. To add an extra special touch, orange juice can be added to the basting mixture.

BARBECUED STEAK

2-2½ lbs. sirloin steak
8 ozs. olive oil
¼ cup soy sauce
*   salt to taste
*   black pepper

1 cup tomato sauce
2 tablespoons brown sugar
1 green pepper, cut in chunks
1 onion, sliced

1. Season steak with salt and pepper. Combine other ingredients, pour over steak.
2. Marinate in refrigerator 4 hours or overnight, turning occasionally. Broil steak. Serves 4.

BEEF LIVER IN BARBECUE SAUCE

1 lb. beef liver cut in ¼" slices
2 tablespoons butter or margarine
1 cup sliced onions
½ cup green sweet pepper, cut up
1 tablespoon vinegar
*   salt and black pepper

1 tablespoon Pickapeppa sauce
1 teaspoon sugar
1 teaspoon prepared mustard
¼ cup tomato ketchup
½ teaspoon hot pepper sauce

1. Start heating oven to 325°F. Cut liver slices in half crosswise. Place half of slices side by side, in covered, shallow baking dish; sprinkle lightly with salt and pepper.
2. Sauté onion and sweet pepper in butter or margarine and arrange half on liver. Mix vinegar with next five ingredients with rest of liver then rest of sauce.
3. Bake uncovered for 10 minutes. Makes 4 servings. The family will need no encouragement to try this dish.

CHRISTMAS HAM WITH BARBECUE SAUCE

1   12-15 lb. ham
1   cup brown sugar

2   tablespoons mustard
1   cup sherry

1.   Preheat oven to 325°F. Bake ham, allowing 25 minutes per pound. When ham is almost done, remove from oven, score and add cloves.
2.   Make a mixture of brown sugar and mustard, then add sherry.
3.   Mixture should be like a thick paste. Coat thickly over ham, then bake for another ½ hour.

JIFFY BARBECUE SAUCE

½ cup tomato ketchup
1 teaspoon dry mustard
1 teaspoon hot pepper sauce
2 teaspoons mango chutney

2 teaspoons Pickapeppa Sauce
* liquid from the can of corn & water to make ¾ cup

Combine all ingredients and pour over pork chops.

MEAT LOAF WITH BARBECUE SAUCE

LOAF
1½ lbs. ground beef
½ lb. ground lean pork

3 strips bacon, cut in small pieces
½ cup bread crumbs

GARNISH
8 bacon strips

SAUCE
2 tablespoons ketchup
¼ teaspoon Worchestershire/ Pickapeppa sauce
½ cup tomato juice
2 eggs
2 tablespoons minced onions

2 tablespoons salt
* parsley sprigs
¼ teaspoon chili powder
1 tablespoon minced onion
2 tablespoons vinegar

1.   Combine all loaf ingredients. Shape into individual loaves (makes 8 loaves).
2.   Wrap a strip of bacon around each loaf.
3.   Simmer sauce ingredients for 15 minutes, then pour over loaves. Bake at 350°F for 45 minutes, basting once or twice during baking.

ORANGE GRILLED FISH

2 lbs. firm white fish

MARINADE

4 tablespoons soy sauce

2 tablespoons tomato ketchup

2 tablespoons chopped parsley

½ cup orange juice

* grated rind of ½ orange

* salt and black pepper

1. Cut the fish into 1" pieces. Mix the ingredients for the marinade together, beating well. Pour over the fish and leave to marinate for 1 hour.
2. Drain the fish and thread on six skewers. Grill over hot coals for about 8 minutes, then turn and grill for a further 7 minutes.
3. Baste with the marinade during cooking. Serves 6.

SHRIMP WITH COLD BARBECUE SAUCE

2 lbs. fresh shrimp

½ cup finely chopped celery

1 stalk scallion

6 tablespoons olive oil

3 tablespoons lemon juice

¼ cup ketchup

1 clove garlic

¼ teaspoon hot pepper sauce

5 tablespoons horseradish

2 tablespoons prepared mustard

¼ teaspoon paprika

¾ teaspoon salt

½ teaspoon white pepper

1. Clean then poach shrimp.
2. To prepare sauce: rub bowl with garlic, then combine other ingredients.
3. Marinate shrimp in sauce for an hour. Serve chilled on a bed of lettuce.

SMOKED PORK CHOPS, BAKED WITH JIFFY BARBECUE SAUCE

6 smoked pork chops

1 can whole kernel corn

1 egg, well beaten

1 cup chopped celery

1 onion, chopped

2 tablespoons oil

1 ounce margarine

1 green sweet pepper, chopped

1. Sauté celery, onion and sweet green pepper in margarine, and mix with corn & egg.
2. Brown chops lightly in oil, drain and arrange in a casserole dish.
3. Cover with the corn mixture and pour sauce all over.
4. Bake covered at 350°F for one hour. Remove cover during last 10 minutes.

SPICY ROAST BEEF BARBECUE

(Roasted Irish potatoes, when done liberally drenched with butter or margarine, and maybe roasted ears of sweet corn, would be perfect accompaniments. To cool things off, how about a big cabbage slaw, dressed with mayonnaise and prinkled with paprika?)

1	(4 - 5 lbs.) Beef rump roast, rolled and tied	½	teaspoon Pimento
½	cup butter	½	teaspoon coriander
1	cup vinegar	¼	teaspoon chili powder
½	teaspoon dry mustard	1	tablespoon lemon juice
1	tablespoon minced onion	⅓	cup brown sugar
1	tablespoon Pickapeppa Sauce	*	salt and pepper to taste

1. Leave roast at room temperature for at least on hour.
2. Start the fire in the barbecue, and let the charcoal bed burn until charcoal turns ash gray in colour.
3. Tap the gray ash from the coals with fire tongs. After you start the fire, skewer the roast on the spit rod, through the centre of the roast (if it is not centred properly, the spit will not turn.) Insert holding forks.
4. When the fire is ready, start to brown the roast. While the roast is browning, combine the sauce ingredients in a saucepan, and heat until the butter melts. Makes about 2 cups. When roast is an even brown on all sides start to baste with the sauce, basting every 20 minutes until done.

(See Cooking Chart)

Pickles & Preserves

BREAD AND BUTTER PICKLES

1 qrt. sliced cucumbers	1 qrt. sliced cucumbers
2 sliced onions	2 sliced onions
1 sliced green pepper	1 sliced green pepper
1 chopped clove garlic	1 chopped clove garlic

1. Place onions, cucumbers, pepper, garlic and salt in a pan. Cover with ice cubes and let stand for 2 hours. Drain.
2. Combine other ingredients and pour over onion mixture. Heat to boil for a few minutes only. Seal while still hot in jars. Makes approximately 4 jars.

CORN RELISH

12 young corn ears	2 teaspoons flour
3 peppers (remove seeds)	4 cups vinegar
1½ cups sugar	4 onions
2 tablespoons salt	* mustard to taste

1. Remove corn from the cob. Put onions and pepper through a mincer and mix with corn. Cover with 3 cups of vinegar.
2. To remaining cup of vinegar add sugar, salt, flour and mustard to make a paste. Add this to vegetable mixture and bring to a slow boil for 30 minutes.
3. Pour into hot jars and seal.

HOT PEPPERS AND SHALLOTS

6 hot peppers	1 clove
2 cups white vinegar	* salt
* shallots to fill 2 jars	* pimento grains

1. Slice peppers and remove seeds.
2. Peel and wash shallots.
3. Fill jars with shallots and hot pepper slices. Boil vinegar with spices and salt.
4. Pour over peppers and shallots and seal.

MANGO CHUTNEY

2 ozs. green ginger	1 oz. garlic powder
2 lbs. brown sugar	2 ozs. salt
1 lb. green mangoes - peeled and sliced	1 sliced hot pepper
1 lb. raisins	1 sliced onion
1 tablespoon soya sauce	

1. Crush the ginger. Mix all ingredients and bring to a boil.
2. Simmer gently until chutney is thick and syrupy.
3. Correct seasoning.

RED DEVIL

6 peppers, seeded and diced	1 teaspoon nutmeg
3 diced onions	* pinch of salt
1 pint vinegar	

1. Put hot peppers and onions through a mincer.
2. Combine with vinegar, nutmeg and salt and bring to a boil.
3. Bottle when cool.

TO PRESERVE FRESH TOMATOES

1. Choose firm, ripe, small tomatoes without blemish.
2. Put them in a jar with a large mouth.
3. Fill jar with oil (corn oil preferably) so that tomatoes are covered with a layer of oil 1" deep. On top of oil pour a little brandy or rum, then seal.

PICKLED WATERMELON

2 lbs. sugar	4 cloves
2 quarts water	1 piece hot pepper
¼ cup salt	* pieces of cinnamon stick (or grated
1 pint vinegar	nutmeg)
* peel of watermelon	

1. Peel off outer green skin of watermelon and chop the white flesh into pieces. Cover with water and salt and simmer until tender.
2. Bring remaining ingredients to a boil for 10 minutes. Add tender melon to this and continue to simmer until melon is transparent. Pack in jars. Makes approx. 4 jars.

VEGETABLE RELISH

6 carrots	1 cucumber
1 pepper, seeds removed	6 olives
2 onions	2 cups water
2 cho-chos	

1. Chop carrots, peppers, onions, cho-chos, cucumbers and olives, add water to cover. Bring to a boil to tenderize.
2. Drain.

DRESSING

½ cup oil	1 tablespoon hot pepper sauce
1 cup vinegar	* salt to taste
2 tablespoons ketchup	

1. Mix dressing and bring to a boil.
2. Pour dressing over the vegetables, which have been packed in sterilized jars.
3. Makes 4 jars.

GARLIC VINEGAR

Steep garlic cloves, which have been pricked with a pin, in vinegar for 10 days. Use for salad dressings.

HERB VINEGARS

Various herb vinegars can be made by loosely packing a jar with a combination of herbs and filling with vinegar. Stand jar in a saucepan of water and bring to a boil slowly. Then allow to cool. After two weeks, vinegar will be ready for use.

PEPPER WINE

Fill ¾ bottle with either cherry or bird peppers. Fill up with sherry or rum. Allow to stand for about one week before using.

ESCOVITCH FISH

RED PEAS SOUP

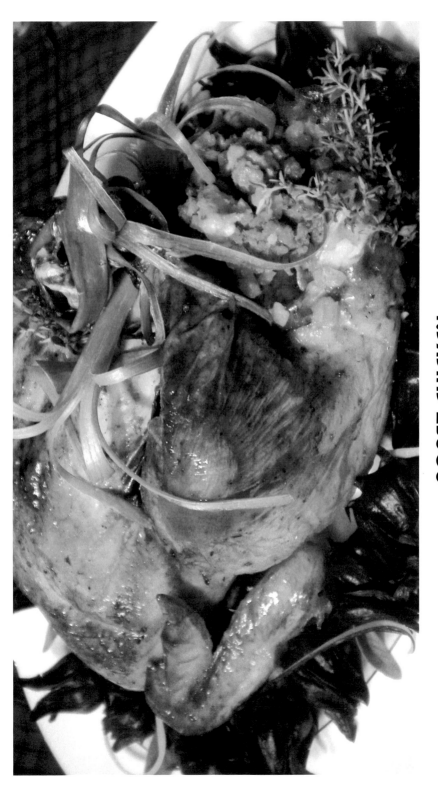

ROAST CHICKEN

GUAVA MOUSSE

Jellies & Jams

PINEAPPLE JAM

| 1 | pineapple | * | nutmeg |
| * | sugar | | **Peel and grate the pineapple.** |

1. To each lb. of pineapple pulp, add ¾ lb. of sugar.
2. Add nutmeg to taste. Boil and stir until mixture thickens and sugar is melted.
3. Seal in jars while hot. Makes approx. 3 jars.

PUMPKIN JAM

3	lbs. pumpkin	1	orange
2	lbs. sugar	*	salt
1	lime		

1. Peel and cut pumpkin into slices, then dice and pack in a jar. Add sugar. Cover and stand for 12 hours.
2. Drain off liquid and boil until syrupy. Add pumpkin, sliced lime and orange.
3. Stir in a pinch of salt. Boil up, and cook until clear.
4. Seal in jars. Makes approx. 6 jars.

TOMATO JAM

8	tomatoes peeled and chopped	2	tablespoons chopped raisins
2	tablespoons lime juice	½	teaspoon all spice
4	cups sugar		

1. Simmer tomatoes for 10 minutes.
2. Add all ingredients except sugar and bring to a boil.
3. Add sugar and continue to boil until sugar melts and mixture thickens. Skim and cool.

SORREL JELLY

2 lbs. sorrel   3 cups granulated sugar
2 cups water

1.   Remove sorrel petals and rinse.
2.   Place sorrel in a deep pot and cover with water, bring to a boil and simmer until tender (about 10 - 15 minutes).
3.   Pour in a strong fine cloth (muslin) and allow to drain. Do not squeeze.
4.   Pour liquid in a heavy pot; add sugar and cook until jelly spins a thread.
5.   Pour in hot sterilized jars and seal immediately. Serves 32. Makes 2 - 8 oz. jars

CALF'S FOOT JELLY

4 calves feet   2 cups sugar
5 qrts. cold water   1 pint sherry
* whites and crushed shells of eggs   ½ teaspoon nutmeg
* juice of 3 limes   ½ cup water
* juice of 1 orange

1.   Clean feet well and put into a pan of cold water. Bring slowly to a boil and simmer for 5 hours. Set aside to cool overnight. In the morning skim jelly from the top and discard sediment on bottom.
2.   Put on heat and melt slowly. Add egg whites beaten to a froth, the crushed shells, nutmeg, sugar and fruit juices. Boil hard for 20 minutes without stirring.
3.   Add 1 cup of water and let come to a boil again. Reduce heat and let simmer covered for about 30 minutes.
4.   Dip a flannel jelly bag into boiling water. Hang it up with a bowl underneath. Pour jelly into bag and let it drip. The bag must not be touched or jelly will cloud.
5.   Turn jelly into a mould. Stir in wine and put in a cool place.

SEA GRAPE JELLY

7 lbs. sea grapes   * sugar
7 pints water

1.   Add grapes to water and bring to a boil. Stir with a wooden spoon and crush fruit while stirring. Boil for about 20 minutes.
2.   Drip through a sieve without stirring.
3.   Measure this juice, and for every cup of liquid, add an equal amount of sugar.
4.   Return sugar and liquid to heat and boil rapidly. Skim.
5.   Boil until a little tested on a plate will jell.
6.   Pour into jars, and cool before sealing.
7.   Makes approx. 4-5 jars.

ORANGE JELLY OR GUAVA JELLY

7 lbs. sliced guavas or
7 cups diced oranges

7 pints water (boil 30 minutes)
* sugar

1. These are made with the same formula as sea-grape jelly (see above).
2. Strain and measure juice in each instance, and add an equal amount of sugar. Boil until liquid jells
3. Pour into jars. Makes approx. 4-5 jars.

BLENDER GRAPEFRUIT MARMALADE

4 grapefruits
2 limes
1½ cups water

5 cups sugar
¹/₈ teaspoon soda
1 oz. gelatin powder

1. Lightly peel and seed grapefruit. Chop two and put into a blender with ½ cup water. Mince. Add soda to this and boil.for 30 minutes.
2. Cut up remaining 2 grapefruits and limes discarding seeds. Add to ½ cup water and mince in blender. Add this to cooked mixture with rest of water and boil for 30 minutes.
3. Add sugar and. stir and boil for 10-15 minutes, being careful to stir frequently to avoid burning and to melt sugar.
4. Add dissolved gelatin to marmalade when it has cooled slightly. Should make 4 jars.

ORANGE MARMALADE

4 large seville oranges
2 teaspoons salt

* sugar

1. Wash oranges and peel lightly. Cut into quarters, removing pips and pulp. Cover pips and pulp with water and let stand overnight. Slice (or cut with scissors) the peel very thinly and add a little salt. Cover with water and soak overnight.
2. The next morning bring peel to a boil and boil until tender. Strain liquid from pips and pulp and add to the fruit mixture. Measure this and add sugar equal to this quantity.
3. Boil up again, simmer and stir until sugar melts and liquid thickens. Be careful not to burn, so at this point cook on a low flame.
4. When mixture jells, skim and remove and pour into jars.

GUAVA CHEESE

* ripe guavas (whatever amount desired)   *** sugar**

1. Wash guavas, cover with water and boil until tender. Rub through a sieve, weigh the pulp, and add an equal quantity of sugar.
2. Boil until mixture shrinks from the sides of pot. Stir all the time to prevent burning.
3. When a little dropped in water forms a ball, pour into a shallow dish. Cool and cut into squares when firm.

LIME CURD

4 limes grated and juiced
1 lb. granulated sugar

4 ozs. butter
4 eggs beaten

1. Combine all ingredients in a double boiler and simmer until sugar dissolves and mixture is thick.
2. Makes 2 jars.

Desserts

AMBROSIA

4 oranges peeled and sliced
1 small shredded coconut
4 tablespoons wine

½ cup pomegranate seeds
* sugar

1. Pile fruit in alternate layers into a bowl, sprinkle with sugar, coconut and wine.
2. End with a layer of pomegranate seeds.

BANANAS IN BATTER

1 oz. sugar
½ oz. butter
9 tablespoons milk
1 teaspoon baking powder
1 egg
3 ripe bananas

½ cup rum
1 tablespoon sugar
1 teaspoon lime juice
8 ozs. flour
* oil

1. Peel bananas and cut into thick chunks.
2. Soak in rum, sugar and lime juice.
3. Mix remaining ingredients except the oil.
4. Dip banana chunks into the batter, using a spoon. Fry lightly in hot oil.

RIPE BANANA PIE

2 sliced bananas
1 package lime jello - prepared
   as instructions

* cherries
* shredded coconut (optional)

1. Place sliced bananas in a pre-baked pie shell.
2. Cover with cooked lime jello mixture. Chill.

BANANA PUDDING

6 ripe crushed bananas
3 tablespoons melted butter
1 glass white wine

¼ lb. sugar
3 beaten egg whites
* vanilla to taste

1. Mix all together and beat until smooth.
2. Put into a soufflé dish, and bake in a 325°F oven until puffy and golden brown on top.
3. Serve at once. The yolk may be used to make a sauce to serve with the pudding.
4. Decorate with cherries and shredded coconut.

CASHEW NUT ICE CREAM

1 cup grape juice
½ cup chopped cashew nuts

1 qrt. vanilla ice cream
* pinch ginger powder

1. Mix the juice, nuts and ginger into the ice cream.
2. Refreeze for about 2 hours.

COCONUT CREAM PIE

1½ cups milk
¾ cup grated coconut
3 eggs, separated
4 tablespoons sugar

1 teaspoon vanilla and a pinch of salt
2 cups flour
1 cup margarine
4 tablespoons ice water - salt to taste

1. Heat milk and set aside. Beat yolks and add sugar, vanilla, salt and coconut.
2. Stir in heated milk and fold in stiffly beaten egg whites.
3. Mix together flour, margarine, water and salt to form a dough.
4. Roll out and line a pie dish. Prick the bottom.
5. Pour in filling and bake for 50 minutes in a 350°F oven.

COCONUT GIZZADAS

1 lb. brown sugar
¼ pint water
1 grated coconut
½ teaspoon nutmeg

2 cups flour
¼ teaspoon salt
¼ cup margarine
* iced water to blend

1. Make a syrup of sugar and water. Add coconut and nutmeg. Mix well.
2. Cool and fill pastry, shells made as follows.
3. Mix flour and salt, cut in margarine and water.
4. Roll out and cut into circles, mould into cases and pinch up edges.
5. Fill with mixture and bake in a 400°F oven until pastry shells are golden brown.

CHRISTMAS CAKE (TRINIDAD BLACK CAKE)

1 lb. prunes, seeded and chopped
1 lb. raisins
1 lb. currants
1 lb. sultanas
¼ lb. mixed peel
½ lb. cherries, chopped in half
¼ lb. chopped almonds
1½ cups cherry brandy
2 cups rum
2 cups or 1 lb. butter

2 cups or 1 lb. sugar (brown or granulated)
10 eggs (large)
2 tsps. grated lime peel
12 tsps. vanilla extract
1 lb. or 4 cups flour
4 tsps. baking powder
2 tsps. ground cinnamon
¼ cup browning or more
1 cup mixture of rum, cherry brandy
   and sherry

1. On the day before or a few days before baking cake, combine prunes, raisins, currants, sultanas, mixed peel, cherries, almonds, cherry brandy and rum.
2. Line three 8" round cake pans with double layers of wax paper.
3. Cream butter and sugar until light and fluffy.
4. Beat in eggs one at a time; add lime peel and vanilla.
5. Combine flour, baking powder and cinnamon; fold into creamed mixture gradually.
6. Add fruit and enough browning to give desired colour; stir well.
7. Put in lined baking pans ¾ full and bake in a preheated oven at 250°F for first hour; reduce heat to 200°F - 225°F for remaining 2 hours or until tester comes out clean.
8. Prick hot cake and soak with a mixture of rum, cherry brandy and sherry. Cover and set aside. As alcohol soaks in pour more and continue to do so for 12 hours.

N.B. Fruit may also be soaked many months before use.

COCONUT MOULD

3 cups coconut cream
1 tin condensed milk

1 tablespoon gelatin powder
¼ cup warm water

1. Dissolve gelatin in warm water. Mix with coconut cream and condensed milk.
2. Heat through to melt gelatin, but do not boil or mixture will curdle.
3. Cool and chill.

PER PERSON

1 egg
1 oz. plain chocolate

1 tablespoon black coffee
1 tablespoon rum

1. Melt chocolate over low heat.
2. Separate eggs, reserving whites, then beat yolks and stir into melted chocolate mixed with coffee and rum.
3. Whip egg whites and fold into mixture. Put into individual glasses and chill.

DUCKUNOO

6	nearly dry corn on cob ears	½	cup raisins
1	cup brown sugar	2	tablespoons spice
1	dry coconut	*	salt, ginger powder

1. Grate corn and coconut. Mix coconut with water to make 2 cups of cream.
2. Add this liquid to remaining ingredients to make a paste.
3. Spoon into squares of banana leaf which have been dipped into boiling water briefly to make pliable. Tie into parcels.
4. Place in boiling water and steam for 45 minutes.

TROPICAL FRUIT SALAD

1	ripe pineapple or melon	* brandy, optional
	variety of diced fruits, as desired	

1. Cut off the top of a ripe pineapple or use a melon cut into 2 parts. Scoop out flesh and mix with diced fruits - as many varieties as desired.
2. Toss with 2 tablespoons brandy if desired.
3. Return to shell and chill. Fresh lychee and mangos can be added for a surprise. Both these fruits are obtainable in the Castleton area.

GUAVA MOUSSE

2	tablespoons water	1	cup tinned guava nectar
1	cup whipped cream	1	tablespoon gelatin powder

1. Dissolve gelatin in water and add to guava nectar.
2. Heat slowly to melt gelatin.
3. Cool slightly before adding the whipped cream.
4. Set in individual glasses. Chill to serve.

GUAVA PIE

CRUST

1½	cups flour	3	tablespoons butter
2	tablespoons sugar	¾	cup milk
1¼	teaspoons baking powder	*	a pinch of salt

1. Mix flour, sugar, baking powder and salt.
2. Cut butter into this and blend until mixture looks like cornmeal. Stir in milk.
3. Knead on a floured board for 1 minute. Divide dough into 2 balls.
4. Roll out bottom crust, cut and fit into a greased pie dish. Put in filling of guava slices with some syrup.
5. Cover with remaining dough. Brush over with milk and make one or two slits in the pastry.
6. Bake in a 350°F oven for about 30 minutes

FILLING

ripe guavas (when in season)
or use tinned guavas

* water
* sugar

1. Peel fresh guavas, cut in half and scoop out seeds.
2. Cover with water, add sugar and boil slowly until fruit is tender and a syrup has formed. Fill crust.

WATERMELON SORBET

5 lbs. seedless watermelon, cut into small chunks (6 cups)
¼ cup sugar
grated peel of 1 lime

½ cup light corn syrup (replace corn syrup with condensed milk to make ice cream)
* pinch of salt

1. Use a blender to puree the watermelon; you will need 4 cups watermelon puree.
2. In a large saucepan, bring 1 cup puree, the sugar and lime peel to a simmer over medium-low heat, stirring until the sugar dissolves; season with salt. Pour in the remaining 3 cups puree, then whisk in the corn syrup until incorporated. Pour the mixture into a 9-inch metal cake pan and freeze until firm, about 4 hours or overnight.
3. Let the frozen puree soften at room temperature for 5 mins. Using a butter knife, break it into 2-inch pieces. Transfer the pieces to a food processor in batches and pulse until smooth. Store the sorbet in a freezer-safe container for up to 1 week. Let stand for 5 mins. before scooping.

MAMMEE APPLE PIE

1 mammee apple
1 8" baked pie shell
2 tablespoons brown sugar

1 cup water
1 tablespoon lime juice
½ teaspoon mixed spices

1. Make a syrup with sugar, water and lime juice.
2. Peel and scrape the fruit, slice and simmer gently in the syrup until tender.
3. Fill the pre-baked crust and sprinkle with spices.
4. Chill and serve with cream - or coconut cream if desired.

PIE CRUST

8 ozs. flour
4 ozs. margarine

* pinch of salt
* cold water

1. Combine flour, margarine and salt. Add 2-3 tablespoons cold water to make a soft dough.
2. Roll out pastry larger than pie dish.
3. Cut to fit, lapping over dish edge slightly.
4. Cut a border and press it around the dampened edges of dish.
5. Bake for ½ hour in 350°F oven. Allow to cool before filling.

LIME PIE

2 egg yolks
4 ozs. condensed milk
¾ cup lime juice
* salt

6 tablespoons sugar
3 egg whites
1 baked pie shell

1. Beat yolks, stir in milk and add lime juice gradually. Beat well.
2. Whip egg whites with a pinch of salt and fold into mixture.
3. Pour into a baked pie shell and cover with meringue made with 3 stiffly beaten egg whites and 6 tablespoons of sugar.
4. Bake in a preheated oven for 10 minutes, or until meringue is a golden colour.

BOMBAY MANGO SPECIAL

1 mango per person

1. Halve the mangoes and take out the seeds.
2. Fill cavities with vanilla ice cream

NASEBERRY PANCAKES

1 cup milk
1 egg
1 egg yolk
1 tablespoon sugar

4 ozs. flour
1 tablespoon butter
5 naseberries

1. Combine first 6 ingredients to make a batter. Then add the naseberries, peeled and crushed.
2. Mix well and drop by the spoonful into a hot, greased fry pan. Brown on both sides.
3. Serve with butter or syrup.

ORANGE ICE BOX DESSERT

2 cups milk
2 tablespoons corn starch
1 cup sugar
4 egg yolks
1 tablespoon gelatin

2 tablespoons cold water
¾ cup orange juice
1 teaspoon orange rind
1 pint whipped cream
* sponge cake slices

1. Heat milk in double boiler. Mix corn starch, sugar and yolks and pour into warm milk. Cook slowly for 10 minutes.
2. Dissolve gelatin into warm water and add juice and rind. Place in refrigerator to chill and thicken.
3. Line a spring form pan with slices of sponge cake. Pour mixture over this and chill.
4. Just before serving top with some whipped cream.

ORANGE SORBET

1½ pts. water
5 ozs. sugar
4 oranges

1 lime
1 glass white wine
1 egg white

1. Bring the sugar and water to a boil, dissolve and reduce.
2. Add the grated rind of 1 orange, and the juice of 4 oranges and 1 lime.
3. Bring to a boil, strain and cool.
4. Semi-freeze. Whisk egg white briskly and add along with wine to mixture.
5. Freeze until mushy and serve in parfait glasses.

OTAHEITE PUDDING

ripe otaheite apples
¾ cup sugar
2 tablespoons butter or margarine

1 teaspoon spice
1 teaspoon baking powder

1. Peel and slice apples. Sprinkle sugar in a greased dish and dot with butter and spice.
2. Arrange apple slices on top.
3. Pour naseberry batter over the slices, or use other batter, adding 1 tsp. of baking powder.
4. Bake at 350°F for 35 minutes.

PICKNEY'S SWEET

½ jar of strawberry jam
* a little water

* whipped cream and chopped nuts

1. Heat jam with water to thin slightly.
2. Pour into glasses.
3. Cool and top with whipped cream and chopped nuts.

MANGO SHERBET

1 sachet vegetable gelatin
2 tbsps. cold water
8 fl ozs. evaporated milk
8 ozs. sugar

8 ozs. moderately crushed mango
1 tsp. vanilla essence
1 egg white, beaten

1. Soften the gelatin in cold water in a cup and stand it over hot water to dissolve.
2. Pour the gelatin into a bowl together with the milk, sugar, crushed mango and vanilla essence. Whip everything together for a few seconds.
3. Pour the mixture into a suitable container and freeze for 1 hour.
4. Remove the sherbet from the freezer and whip until smooth.
5. Beat the egg white until it is frothy, then fold it into the sherbet.
6. Return the sherbet to the freezer to freeze until firm. Serves 4.

RUM COFFEE JELLY

2 tablespoons gelatin
2 cups of hot strong coffee
½ cup sugar
2 tablespoons lime juice

3 tablespoons rum
2 cups sour cream
1 cup brown sugar
½ teaspoon cinnamon

1. Soften gelatin in ½ cup of cold water.
2. Add hot coffee and sugar and stir until gelatin is dissolved. Add lime juice and rum.
3. Pour into an 8" dish and chill until firm. Cut into cubes and serve a sauce made by beating together sour cream, sugar and cinnamon until sugar dissolves.

CORNMEAL PUDDING

2 cups coconut milk
4 cups water
½ cup margarine
½ cup raisins
2 cups brown sugar
3 cups cornmeal

½ cup flour
½ tablespoon cinnamon
1½ teaspoons salt
2 teaspoons vanilla
2½ cups milk

FOR SOFT TOP
1 cup coconut milk
½ cup brown sugar

½ teaspoon cinnamon

1. Put coconut milk, water, margarine, raisins and sugar to boil.
2. Combine cornmeal, flour, cinnamon, nutmeg, salt and vanilla and add 2½ cups milk to soften.
3. Add to the boiling liquid and stir briskly.
4. Lower flame and boil for ten minutes, stirring continuously.
5. Pour into a greased baking tin, then top mixture of coconut milk, sugar and cinnamon.
6. Bake at 350°F in a preheated oven for about 55-60 minutes.
7. Remove from oven, cool and serve.

May be served with rum sauce (See Dressings & Sauces)

A TASTY, LOW-CHOLESTEROL RECIPE FOR PASTRY

1 cup flour
½ teaspoon salt
¼ cup vegetable oil

2 tablespoons skimmed milk powder
mixed in water

1. Mix flour and salt. Combine oil and milk and pour over flour.
2. Stir with a fork till smooth.
3. Shape into a ball, flatten and wrap with a sheet of waxed paper. Chill.
4. Peel off the paper and roll out. Use as desired.

BASIC BREAD DOUGH

2½ cups flour
1 teaspoon dry yeast
½ cup warm water
* pinch of salt

2 tablespoons melted butter
5 tablespoons cold milk
1 egg beaten into 1 tablespoon milk
2 tablespoons flour

1. Sift flour and salt. Dissolve yeast in a cup of warm water. Combine with butter and milk. Cover bowl and set aside to rise for 2 hours.
2. Put 2 tablespoons flour on table and pat dough to ½" thickness. Cut dough into 2 pieces and roll from corner to corner like a jelly roll.
3. Brush with egg and milk and slash surface at intervals. Place in bread loaf pans and bake 15 minutes in a fast oven, then lower to 350°F and bake 15 minutes more.

BANANA BREAD

1 cup sugar
¼ cup margarine or butter
3 crushed, ripe bananas
2 cups flour

1 unbeaten egg
1 teaspoon baking powder
½ teaspoon soda
* vanilla flavouring

1. Cream sugar and butter. Add bananas and mix well. Add egg and dry ingredients and vanilla. Beat well.
2. Bake in a greased, paper-lined loaf tin at 350°F for 50 minutes. This freezes well.

EGG BREAD

2 teaspoons sugar
2 eggs (beaten)
1 egg yolk
1 pack yeast

4 cups flour
1 cup warm water
1 tablespoon oil

1. Soak yeast in warm water for 5 minutes. Sift flour, salt and sugar together. Add 1 ½ cups flour to the yeast and beat. Cover and allow to rise about 30 minutes.
2. Add the 2 eggs and remaining flour and oil to dough. Knead. Place in a bowl to rise for 2 hours.
3. Knead dough again. Divide into 3 strands and braid, turning ends under. Place on a greased sheet and let rise for 1 hour.
4. Preheat 400°F. Brush the top with egg yolk. Bake for 10-15 minutes. Reduce oven to 350°F and bake for 30 minutes. Bread should be golden brown on top.

ORANGE BREAD

1 cup minced orange peel
1 cup orange juice
2½ cups of sugar
1 beaten egg
3½ cups flour

1 cup milk
½ teaspoon melted butter
2 teaspoons baking powder
* pinch of salt

1. Combine orange peel and juice and boil until peel is tender. Add 1½ cups sugar, and boil slowly until thick and syrupy. Cool.
2. Mix egg, 1 cup sugar, butter and milk. Sift flour with baking powder and salt. Add mixture and stir. Add orange mixture to dough and blend well.
3. Pour into 2 loaf tins which have been greased and floured. Bake at 350°F for 40 minutes. This is great when toasted with cheese spread.

EASTER SPICE BUNS

3 cups flour
¼ tsp. baking powder
1 tbsp. baking soda
2 cups hot water
1½ cups brown sugar
4 tbsps. margarine
1 lb. raisins
¼ lb. mixed dried fruit

¼ tsp. molasses
¼ tsp. salt
1 tsp. cinnamon
1 tsp. nutmeg
½ tsp. ground allspice
3 tbsps. water
3 tbsps. sugar

1. Preheat oven to 325°F.
2. In a large bowl, combine flour, baking powder, and baking soda.
3. In a medium saucepan, bring water to a boil.
4. Add sugar, stirring until dissolved.
5. Lower heat; add margarine, raisins, mixed fruit, molasses, salt, and spices.
6. Let simmer for 10 minutes.
7. Remove from heat and let cool.
8. Add cooled liquid to flour mixture. Stir and blend, but do not over mix.
9. To glaze buns before baking, combine water and sugar and brush mixture onto buns.
10. Pour batter into a 5" x 9" greased loaf pan.
11. Bake for 1 to 1½ hours.

PUMPKIN BREAD

3 cups sugar
1 cup oil
4 eggs

1 cup boiled, crushed pumpkin
3 cups flour

1. Grease and flour 2 loaf pans. Mix all ingredients together in a large bowl. Pour into pans.
2. Bake 1 hour at 350°F. Cool for 10 minutes in the pan. Wrap in foil and store in the refrigerator.

SODA BREAD

1 lb. flour	2 tablespoons soda
1 cup warm milk	1 tablespoon salt

1. Mix all ingredients and knead to a soft dough. Divide into 2 loaves.
2. Brush with milk and dredge lightly with flour. Bake for 30-40 minutes or until lightly brown on top in a 425°F oven.

BAKING POWDER BISCUITS

2 cups flour	¾ cup milk
2½ teaspoons baking powder	* salt
⅓ cup margarine	

1. Sift together flour and baking powder. Cut margarine into the flour mixture with a fork. Add milk and salt. Knead and roll out to ½" thickness.
2. Cut into circles and bake on an ungreased sheet for 15 minutes in a hot oven, at 400-450°F.

BANANA MUFFINS

6½ ozs. flour	1 egg
1 tablespoon corn flour	3 crushed bananas
2 ozs. butter	1 teaspoon baking powder
3 ozs. sugar	½ teaspoon soda and a pinch of salt

1. Sift together, flour, corn flour, baking powder, soda and salt.
2. Cream butter and sugar. Beat egg and mix into creamed mixture.
3. Add dry ingredients and crushed bananas alternately. Do hot beat, but mix in well.
4. Bake in greased muffin containers in 400°F oven for 20 minutes.

CORN BREAD

¼ cup wheat flour	1 large eggs
1 cup cornmeal	14¾ ozs. can creamed corn
1 tsp. salt	8¼ ozs. crushed pineapple, well drained
1 lb. unsalted butter, room temperature	1 cup shredded Monterey Jack Cheese
1 cup sugar	

1. Preheat oven to 325°F. Grease and flour an 8" x 13" baking pan.
2. Mix all dry ingredients.
3. Beat butter and sugar in a mixing bowl until mixture is pale yellow and forms a ribbon.
4. Add eggs one at a time, mixing well, then add corn, pineapple and cheese.
5. Stir in the mixed flours, salt and baking powder. Bake about one hour until golden brown. Yields: 12 servings.

BAPS

1 lb. flour	1 teaspoon sugar
½ teaspoon salt	½ pint of warm milk
2 ozs. margarine	2 teaspoons yeast powder

1. Combine flour and salt in a bowl. Rub margarine into flour mixture until mixture looks like fine crumbs.
2. Dissolve yeast into warm milk. Make a well in the flour mixture then stir in yeast then mixture into the well along with sugar. Mix with a wooden spoon to form a soft dough.
3. The dough should not be sticky. Knead until smooth and silky. Cover with a damp dish towel and allow to rise approximately 30 minutes
4. Punch down the risen dough. Turn out onto a floured board and knead for a few seconds.
5. Roll dough into a 'fat' rope size and cut into even pieces. Form each piece in oval shapes and lightly brush with milk. Sift flour over each bap.
6. Set onto greased baking sheets and let rise for approximately 30 minutes, just before baking sift another fine layer of flour over the baps, then press your thumb into the centre of each. This helps them remain flat instead of baking into a domed roll. Preheat oven at 400°F and bake for 15 minutes.

COCONUT BAKE

1 lb. all purpose flour	3 ozs. grated coconut
3 tsps. baking powder	4 ozs. butter
½ teaspoon salt	1½ ozs. vegetable shortening
2 tablespoons brown sugar	½ pint coconut milk

1. Sift flour, baking powder and salt into a medium bowl.
2. Add brown sugar and grated coconut, and rub in the shortening.
3. Slowly add coconut milk and mix to form a dough.
4. Knead for approximately 5 minutes or until dough is smooth. Leave to rest for 1 hour.
6. Shape into a ball and roll out flat approximately 1 inch thick.
7. Preheat the oven 350°F.
8. Place on a greased baking sheet and bake for 20-30 minutes or until golden brown.

CASSAVA PONE

(Pone can also be made with a combination of pumpkin and sweet potato or cornmeal.)

2 cups grated cassava	¼ tsp. ground nutmeg
1 cup grated coconut	1 tsp. cinnamon
1 cup brown sugar	* Pinch of fresh ground ginger
4 tbs. butter	1 tsp. vanilla extract
½ cup evaporated milk	¼ cup raisins, finely chopped

1. Preheat oven to 250°F or 280°C
2. Put all ingredients in a large bowl and mix well.
3. Put the mixture into a greased rectangular 8-inch baking dish and bake in oven until golden brown and firm.

CARROT BREAD & LEMON GLAZE FROSTING

2 eggs
½ cup of flour
1 cup of walnuts
¼ cup of sugar
1 cup of salad oil

1 teaspoon of vanilla
½ teaspoon of salt
1½ teaspoon of cinnamon
½ cup of carrot pieces
1½ teaspoon of baking soda

LEMON GLAZE FROSTING INGREDIENTS:
1 tablespoon of milk
½ cups of icing sugar

2½ cups of lemon juice

1. Heat the oven to 350°F and grease 9" x 5" loafpan. Sift together the flour, baking soda, salt and cinnamon into large mixing bowl. Set aside.
2. Chop the nuts in blender or with a sharp knife. Add to dry ingredients. Mix sugar, eggs and vanilla until smooth in blender.
3. Add the carrot pieces to mixture in blender and liquefy. Pour over dry ingredients and mix only until dry ingredients are moistened.
4. Pour in a pan and bake for 1 hr. or until tester comes out clean. Cool for 5 minutes in a pan then cool before frosting with lemon glaze.
5. Method to Make Lemon Glaze Frosting:
   Put all the ingredients in blender and process until sugar is liquefied. Pour over the top of bread spreading with a spatula. Frosting will drizzle over bread.

PUDDING AND SOUSE

2 large mixing bowls
2 large saucepans
Grater
Pork (any part that you like,
  Bajans use the head, tails and feet!)
Sweet potato
Limes
Sweet peppers
2 Onions

Scotch bonnet red peppers
Salt
Parsley, Thyme
Cucumber
Chives
Oil
Sugar
Butter

1. Whatever part of the pig you have decided to use, as described above, you need to clean it and boil it in salt water.
2. To make the pudding, you grate the sweet potato into a mixing bowl, add a pinch of sugar and salt, then add 2 ounces of butter and 2 teaspoons of oil. Chop the chives and thyme and add to the bowl.
3. Grate 2 onions and add half to the bowl. Save the other half for the pickle. Now set this bowl aside to absorb the flavour while you prepare the pickle.
4. To make the pickle you need to grate the cucumber and sweet peppers.
5. Now chop up the parsley. Then taking great care, usually wearing rubber gloves slice up half a scotch bonnet pepper into very small pieces. Wash your hands immediately and do not touch your eyes; scotch bonnet peppers can really burn the skin.
6. Now add your remaining onion to the bowl and then squeeze lime juice and salt to your mixing bowl with the cucumber, sweet peppers, scotch bonnet peppers and parsley.
7. By now your pork should be cooked, so drain off the salt water and now sprinkle with lime juice.
8. Now go back to your pudding mixture and put in a grease-proof oven dish and bake in the oven until cooked.

BULLAS

3 cups flour	2 ozs. water
8 ozs. brown sugar	1 teaspoon baking powder
2 ozs. melted butter	

1. Make a syrup of water and sugar. Sift together dry ingredients and add syrup and melted butter.
2. Turn on to a floured board and pat into ¼ inch thickness.
3. Cut into circles. Place on a greased tin and bake for 20 minutes in a 400°F oven.

CASSAVA BAMMY

2 lbs. sweet cassavas

1. Scrape the cassavas and grate. Squeeze out the juice, letting the flour remain. Rub through this flour to remove all lumps.
2. Put a thick-bottomed pan over a low heat and when hot, pour in the cassava flour. When it sets at the bottom, turn over and let the other side set. Scrape to remove any scorching.
3. Bammies may be moistened with a little milk and baked in an oven or browned under grill, or fry them in a pan with a little bacon fat. Each bammy should be about 5" - 6" in diameter and about ½-¾ inch thick.

CASSAVA PUFFS

1 lb. sweet cassava	1 teaspoon baking powder
1 tablespoon margarine	1 teaspoon salt
1 beaten egg	

1. Peel cassavas and boil until tender with some salt. Crush while still hot. Add margarine, baking powder and beaten egg and beat.
2. Drop by spoonfuls into muffin tins which have been greased. Bake for 15 minutes in hot oven. Puffs may also be fried.

JAMAICAN BUN

1 lb. flour	6 ozs. currants
2 ozs. butter	½ lb. brown sugar
2 ozs. margarine	½ teaspoon nutmeg
2 ozs. raisins	½ teaspoon baking powder
2 ozs. mixed peel	* enough milk to make a batter
2 eggs	

1. Blend butter and margarine into flour. Add baking powder, sugar and nutmeg.
2. Add fruit to flour.
3. Beat the eggs and pour into the dry mixture, adding enough milk to make a batter.
4. Pour into a greased loaf tin and bake 1½ hours in a slow oven for about 300°F.
5. Chopped cherries and some lime rind may be added to the mixture if desired.

COCONUT LOAF CAKE

½	cup butter	2	eggs
1½	cups sugar	4	teaspoons baking powder
2²/₃	cups flour	1	cup grated coconut
¾	cup milk	1	teaspoon vanilla

1. Cream butter and half of the sugar.
2. Beat eggs with rest of sugar and combine the mixture.
3. Mix in flour and baking powder adding milk alternately with the dry ingredients.
4. Add coconut and vanilla.
5. Bake for 1 hour in a 350°F oven.

GUAVA LAYER CAKE

½	lb. margarine	2	teaspoons baking powder
1	cup sugar	¼	teaspoon nutmeg
2	eggs	½	teaspoon vanilla
2	cups flour	*	stewed guava slices, or use tinned
1	cup milk		

1. Cream margarine, sugar and eggs. Beat well.
2. Add flour, baking powder and nutmeg. Pour in milk to which vanilla has been added.
3. Bake in two 9" layer tins for 30 minutes in a 350°F oven.
4. Cool and remove from pans. Spread guava slices between the layers.
5. Sprinkle sugar lightly on top. Stewed mangoes may be used in the same manner.

ORANGE CAKE

3	oranges	½	teaspoon soda and a tip of salt
2	eggs	1	cup butter
¾	cup sugar	¼	cup grated orange rind
2	cups flour		

1. Squeeze juice from oranges to make 1 cup and reserve for use.
2. Cream butter and sugar, and add eggs one at a time, beating continuously.
3. Add flour, salt and soda, which have been sifted together.
4. Continue to beat the mixture. Add ¼ cup of orange rind and the juice.
5. Pour into a greased 13" x 9" pan and bake in a moderate oven until firm.

RUM CAKE

½ cup butter
1 cup sugar
3 beaten eggs
¼ teaspoon salt
½ teaspoon baking powder
3 cups flour
* mixed spices

¼ cup milk
¼ cup molasses
2 cups peanuts (crushed)
1 lb. raisins
½ cup rum
* pinch of soda

1. Cream butter, sugar and eggs.
2. Mix flour, baking powder, salt and spices. Add this to butter mixture and blend.
3. Add milk, soda and molasses, and add lastly crushed nuts, raisins and rum.
4. Bake in a loaf tin 300°F for 2 hours.

MANGO & COCONUT PUFF PASTRY PIE

Flesh of 1 coconut grated
2 firm ripe mangoes (or two tins of mangoes, well drained)
450g (1 lb.) puff pastry

1 egg
50 g (2 ozs.) 4 tbsps. caster sugar
¼ tsp. grated nutmeg

1. Break the coconut into large pieces and remove the flesh carefully with a knife. Grate the flesh on a hand grater or blend to medium consistency in a blender or food processor a little at a time at high speed. Put the grated coconut in a bowl, add the almond essence, 2 tablespoons of caster sugar, and grated nutmeg. Mix well and set aside.
2. Peel the mangoes and slice them into small pieces. Put them in a bowl, sprinkle with two tablespoons sugar and set to one side.
3. Preheat oven to 200°C (400°F).
4. Meanwhile, roll out the puff pastry to half-inch thickness and line an 8 inch x 2 inch flan dish with it. Leave enough to make the top of the pie.
5. Spread a layer of half the coconut in the lined flan dish, follow with a layer of half the mango, then another layer of the remainder of the coconut, finishing with a final layer of the remaining mango.
6. Roll out the rest of the pastry to make the top of the pie. Pattern with a knife, brush with honey and bake in the oven for thirty to thirty five minutes. Serve hot or cold on its own or with cream.

KATIE'S SHORT BREAD

1 oz. sugar
4 ozs. butter

2½ ozs. flour
2½ ozs. cornflour (corn starch)

1. Cream butter and sugar. Add flour and cornflour and blend thoroughly.
2. Put through a cookie tube or drop by spoonfuls onto a greased sheet.
3. Bake for 10 minutes in a 375°F oven. Sprinkle with sugar.

COCONUT COOKIES

¾ cup sugar
¼ lb. butter
1½ cups flour

1 tsp. baking powder
1½ cups grated coconut
1 beaten egg

1. Cream butter and sugar. Add flour and baking powder.
2. Mix well then add grated coconut and egg.
3. Mix to a paste. Drop onto a greased cookie sheet by teaspoonsful.
4. Bake at 350°F for 15 minutes. Makes approx. 2 doz.

GUAVA JELLY COOKIES

4 ozs. butter
2 ozs. sugar
1 egg yolk
½ teaspoon vanilla
4 ozs. flour

1 egg white
3 tablespoons chopped nuts
3 tablespoons guava jelly
* pinch of salt

1. Cream butter and sugar and beat in yolk and vanilla. Combine flour and salt and
    add to mixture.
2. Divide and shape into balls. Roll in egg white and then in nuts. Press a hole into
    each cookie and insert guava jelly.
3. Bake with jelly uppermost, on a sheet for 20 minutes, in a moderate oven. Makes
    approx.1 doz.

SWEET POTATO COOKIES

1½ cups flour
2 tablespoons brown sugar
4 teaspoons baking powder
5 tablespoons butter

1 cup crushed, boiled, sweet potato
½ cup of milk
* cinnamon

1. Combine all except milk and potatoes and mix until crumbly. Stir in crushed pota-
    toes and milk.
2. Spoon batter onto a sheet.
3. Bake in a quick oven.
4. Split and serve with honey and butter. Makes approx. 1 doz.

Beverages

MATRIMONY

3 star apples	4 tablespoons condensed milk
2 oranges	* nutmeg

1. Remove star apple pulp. Peel orange and remove sections, discarding seeds.
2. Mix together, sweeten with condensed milk, and flavour with grated nutmeg. Chill.

NASEBERRY NECTAR

8 naseberries peeled and seeded	1 cup water
1 cup sugar	* juice of 1 orange

Put all ingredients through a blender, strain and serve chilled.

PLANTATION RUM PUNCH

3 ozs. any rum	1 teaspoon honey
1 oz. lime juice	* nutmeg

Mix together and pour over cracked ice. Add a sprinkle of nutmeg.

SORREL APPETIZER

1 lb. prepared sorrel	6 pints boiling water
2 ozs. grated green ginger	

1. Mix ingredients together, cover and leave overnight.
2. Strain and add rum and sugar to taste.
3. Serve over crushed ice.

SOURSOP PUNCH

1 ripe soursop
4 glasses water

* condensed milk to taste
* vanilla or rum to flavour

1. Peel and crush soursop, removing seeds.
2. Stir in water and strain.
3. Add milk and flavouring. Serve ice cold.

STAR APPLE APPETIZER

6 star apples (use pulp only)
2 tablespoons rum
2 tablespoons sugar

2 teaspoons lime juice
* angostura bitters

1. Cut star apples in half, remove pulp and mix with rum, sugar and lime juice.
2. Add a few drops of angostura bitters. Serve chilled in fruit glasses.

(For a full range of non-alcoholic beverages see the book CARIBBEAN COCKTAILS & MIXED DRINKS by Mike Henry.)

BANANA MILKSHAKE

2 ripe bananas
1 pint milk (cold)

1 scoop vanilla ice cream
½ teaspoon vanilla

1. Puree the bananas in a blender. Add the cold milk, ice cream and vanilla.
2. Blend well and serve in two tall glasses with straws.
3. If the milkshake is very thick, it can be served over cracked ice.

CHRISTMAS CITRUS PUNCH

6 cups grapefruit juice
5 cups ortanique juice
3 cups orange juice
2 bottles soda water

¾ cup honey
1 whole orange, unpeeled
12 cloves

1. Stick the cloves into the orange and bake in a warm oven until hard. Put the honey in a large bowl and add the fruit juices gradually, stirring so that the honey is completely dissolved. Add the baked orange. Allow the mixture to stand for two hours at least.
2. When ready to serve, place a block of ice in a large bowl and pour the punch over it. Use a ladle to pour the punch over the ice repeatedly until it is completely chilled. Add the soda water and serve.
3. Rum can be added to this punch while it is standing. It can also be garnished with sprigs of mint.

JAMAICAN GINGER BEER

¼ lb. root ginger
2 lbs. sugar
1 oz. yeast

1 lime
½ oz. cream of tartar
6 quarts boiling water

1. Grate ginger and place in a large bowl. Add the lime thinly sliced and cream of tartar. Pour the boiling water over all and allow to stand.
2. In a separate bowl, mix yeast with one cup sugar. Add ½ cup lukewarm water to make a smooth paste.
3. When the ginger mixture is lukewarm, add the yeast and sugar. Stir well. Cover. Let stand for 2-3 days. Skim and strain, then add the sugar, stirring well until it is dissolved.
4. Pour into bottles and let the ginger beer stand at room temperature for three or four days more. Serve chilled. Rum can be added at the bottling stage, if desired.

ENGLISH-SPEAKING

TRINIDAD & TOBAGO

Crab and callaloo is generally considered the national dish of Trinidad and Tobago; it is often prepared for Sunday lunch.

Crab and Callaloo

12 taro (dasheen or callaloo) leaves
¼ pound salted beef or salted pork (or
       ½ lb. seasoned chicken feet)
8 okras
4 stalks chive
2 sprigs thyme
½ cup chopped onion

1 tsp. finely chopped garlic
2 crabs, cleaned and broken in pieces
2 cups coconut milk
2 cups hot water
1 tsp. cooking butter
* 1 whole hot pepper (if being used,
       should be added before boiling)

1. Strip the stalks and midribs from the leaves.
2. Wash and cut leaves and soft stalk, and discard remainder.
3. Soak and cut salted beef or salted pork into bite-sized pieces.
4. Cut okra, chives and thyme into small pieces.
5. In a large pot, put callaloo leaves, salted meat, okra, chive, thyme, onion, garlic, crab, coconut milk and water.
6. Bring to a boil; reduce heat, cover and simmer for 30 minutes or more until everything is soft and cooked.
7. Swizzle or beat with a hand beater.
8. Add cooking butter and stir well.
9. Add salt and pepper to taste.

Pelau

2½ cups of rice (brown rice optional)
½ stick butter
1 onion, chopped
1 garlic clove, chopped
1 lb. whole chicken, chopped into parts
1 16 oz. can pigeon peas
2 stems fresh thyme, cut
2 stems escallion, chopped

4 tablespoons brown sugar
4 tablespoons fry oil
2 tbsps. curry powder
1 inch piece of stick of cinnamon
½ teaspoon salt
1 pack sason seasoning
* black pepper
* garlic powder

1. Grate the coconut, press out all liquid, then strain to remove all grated husk from the liquid. Set the coconut liquid or milk aside.
2. Wash and clean the chopped chicken, using lime and/or vinegar, remove the fat.
3. Season the chicken using the garlic, garlic powder, black pepper, chopped onions, escallion, cinnamon, sason seasoning and thyme, then set aside.
3. In a pot, place the fry oil and sugar, under a medium flame. Let the sugar brown for 3 to 4 minutes. It should be golden brown. Next, place the chicken in the pot and sauté, let it cook for approximately 10 to 15 minutes or until chicken is brown. Turn constantly, so that it doesn't stick.
4. Add rice to the sautéd chicken and spices, let it brown for 3 to 5 minutes. Slowly add the coconut milk, 2 cups at a time. Add the salt and cover the pot tightly. Let the ingredients cook under a low flame for another 15 to 20 minutes or until the liquid has evaporated, and the rice is soft not mushy.
5. As the rice cooks, if it is still hard, add more coconut milk . As you add coconut milk, add more seasonings and salt to taste. After the rice is cooked, just prior to the end of the cooking process, add the butter, pigeon peas and sweet corn (optional). Make sure you drain the water out of the peas and corn before adding it to the cooking process. Let all ingredients simmer for another 5 minutes. Fluff with a fork and serve hot.

BARBADOS

The national dish of Barbados is cou-cou and flying fish. Cou-cou is made out of corn-meal and okra. It may be served with any type of fish, vegetables, rice or pasta.

Flying Fish

6 deboned flying fish (or any filleted white fish)
   Juice of one lime
1 onion, chopped
⅓ cup green onions, chopped
2 cloves garlic, minced
½ hot pepper, chopped

½ tsp. ground thyme
½ tsp. ground cloves
½ tsp. salt
½ tsp. black pepper
* Oil for frying
* Bread crumbs or flour

1. Wash fish and place in bowl.
2. Combine lime juice, onion, green onions, garlic, hot pepper, thyme, cloves, salt and black pepper. Marinate fish in this mixture.
3. Heat oil in saucepan, coat fish in breadcrumbs or flour and fry until brown or for 5 to 10 minutes. Serve with cou-cou, vegetables or rice.

Cou-Cou

4 okras
4 cups water
2 cups cornmeal

2 cups cold water
1 tsp. salt
1 tbsp. butter

1. Put water to boil in a medium-sized pot. Thinly slice okra and add to boiling water. Cook for 10 to 12 minutes, until soft. Lower the heat.
2. Meanwhile, combine cornmeal with cold water and mix well.
3. Add corn mixture to the okra. Add salt. Mix well and cook on low, stirring constantly with a flat wooden spoon or "cou-cou stick".
4. The cou-cou will be ready when it's fairly stiff, and it clean breaks away from the sides of the pot.
5. Place the cou-cou in a serving dish and put the butter on top.

GRENADA

The national dish of Grenada is called 'oil down'. It is a very simple, delicious and robust dish, which is extremely popular at local "cook-ups".

"Oil Down"

8 ozs. salt meat
1 large or 2 small breadfruit,
       cut into 4 or 6 sections
8 ozs. cooked salt fish, flaked
1 whole chili
2 sprigs thyme

2 chives
1 stick celery, chopped or
       ½ teaspoon celery seeds
2¾ pints coconut milk
* salt

1. Soak meat overnight in cold water, drain.
2. Remove the breadfruit core and peel. In a saucepan, put alternate layers of breadfruit, meat and fish.
3. Tie chili, thyme and chives together and add to the pan with celery and coconut milk.
4. Cover tightly and bring to a boil, reduce heat and simmer for about 45 - 50 minutes until everything is cooked and tender.
5. When cooked, the liquid should all be absorbed and the stew oily. Remove herbs before serving and add salt to taste.

Banana Ice Cream

4 eggs
½ cup sugar
2 cups milk, scalded
1½ teaspoons vanilla extract

½ teaspoon ground nutmeg
4 very ripe bananas, peeled and
       mashed

1. Combine the eggs and sugar and beat lightly. Stir in the scalded milk and pour the mixture into the top half of a double boiler set over hot water.
2. Cook, stirring constantly, until the custard thickens and coats the spoon.
3. Cool, stir in the vanilla and nutmeg, and combine with the mashed bananas in an electric blender or food processor.
4. Puree, pour into a shallow pan, cover, and freeze for about 2 hours in the freezer compartment of your refrigerator.
5. Remove from the freezer, beat well, and return to the freezer until set or freeze in an ice cream maker according to the manufacturer's directions.

Antigua & Barbuda

The national dish of Antigua and Barbuda is Fungee and Pepperpot. It is normally prepared either as a breakfast meal or main entree.

Fungee

2 cups cornmeal
3 cups water
   salt to taste

3 ochroes (cut into pieces)
2 tablespoons of butter

1. Bring water to boil with the ochroes until they are cooked.
2. Remove 2 cups of water to a pan, add the cornmeal to the remaining boiling water.
3. Using a wooden spoon, mix the corn meal and crush to the side of the pan to remove lumps. Add water when necessary.
4. When the mixture leaves the bottom of the pan, remove from the fire.
5. Place butter in a small bowl, place a large spoonful of fungee in the bowl and roll to a ball. Serve hot with pepperpot; stewed or fried fish.
6. Fungee can be left overnight. Sliced and dried and used with syrup or jam for breakfast.

Pepperpot

Pepperpot is a stew containing squash, spinach, eggplant, peas, pumpkin, ochroes, salted meats and dumplings.

4 eddo leaves (cut up)
4 eggplants (diced or antrobers)
2 teaspoons of margarine,
4 diced ochroes
* Salt and pepper to taste;
* Bunch of chive and thyme (pounded);
2 onions (chopped);
2 cups of green peas (cooked)
1 lb. spinach chopped;

2 tomatoes sliced;
1 cup diced pumpkin
1 cup diced squash
2 teaspoons of oil
1 lb. salt pork, pig snout or pigs feet
   (cut in pieces)
2 teaspoons of ketchup
1 lb. salt beef or 1lb. other fresh meat
   optional

1. Cook the meats then add the vegetables except the green peas, then add the seasoning.
2. Cook the peas in a small amount of salt water, then remove the vegetables.
3. Chop well and return to fire.
4. When cooked, serve hot with fungee. Dumplings may be added to the mixture.

Tortola

Fungee & Fish

Fungee is prepared as above. Fish is normally steamed, and the type of fish used depends mainly on availability. However, only seawater fish is used.

BERMUDA

The most popular dish in Bermuda is fish chowder. Sherry peppers and black rum may be added to this dish, as they lend a distinctive Bermuda flavour.

FISH CHOWDER

2 lbs. of any type of white fish meat
1 qrt. water
1 minced onion
2 diced carrots

1 diced potato
2 diced tomatoes
* salt and pepper to taste
* sherry, optional

1. Boil fish in water until tender. Remove all bones and strain the liquid.
2. Stir diced vegetables into fish stock with seasonings. When cooked add some flaked fish meat and sherry to taste.

ST. LUCIA

St. Lucia's national dish is Green Figs and Saltfish Pie, usually prepared as a breakfast meal.

Green Figs & Saltfish Pie

2 lbs. green figs
1 lb. saltfish
½ lb. cheese
½ cup milk
1 tbsp. lime juice

2 sweet peppers
2 tomatoes, thinly sliced
1 onion sliced
½ tsp. black pepper
1 tsp. bread crumbs

1. Boil the green figs until tender. Peel and crush with fork while still hot and sprinkle with lime juice to prevent darkening.
2. Soak the fish in boiling water to remove most of the salt.
3. Remove the skin and bones; shred fish. Press half of the crushed fig in a greased baking pie dish.
4. Sprinkle half of shredded fish on fig. Spread half of sweet peppers (cut into thin strips) onion, tomatoes, cheese and black pepper.
5. Repeat layer - beginning with green fig and ending with grated cheese and black pepper.
6. Top with milk and sprinkle with breadcrumbs. Bake in an oven at 180°C, for 30-40 minutes or until the cheese has melted and is golden brown.

GUYANA

'Garlic Pork' is one of the most popular dishes in Guyana and is a traditional Guyanese Christmas dish.

Garlic Pork

¼ pound garlic, chopped
1 teaspoon dried thyme
* salt and freshly ground pepper
4 pounds boneless pork leg or shoulder

1 tablespoon lime juice
2 cups white vinegar
* vegetable oil for frying

1. Mix the garlic and thyme together in a small bowl. Add salt and pepper to taste. Set aside.
2. Wash the pork well with the lime juice and dice into small cubes. Place the pork in a large saucepan, cover with water, and parboil for about 30 minutes.
3. Remove the pork, drain, and discard the water. Rub the garlic mixture over the pork.
4. Place the cubed pork in a large jar or casserole and pour on the vinegar to cover. Cover and refrigerate for 1 to 2 days.
5. Remove from container, drain, and pat dry with paper towels.
6. Heat the oil in a deep fryer or tall saucepan and deep fry the meat until tender, about 10 to 15 minutes.
7. Serve hot as a main course with rice and vegetables or as a snack or appetizer.

ST. VINCENT & THE GRENADINES

'Buljol' is a very popular dish in St. Vincent and the Grenadines and is usually served on a Saturday or Sunday morning.

Buljol

½ lb. salt fish or salted codfish
2 large tomatoes, finely chopped
½ tsp. fresh hot pepper, chopped
1 onion, finely chopped or sliced

1 sweet pepper (green pepper), finely chopped
1-2 tbsp. olive oil

1. Break fish in pieces and place in saucepan with cold water.
2. Gradually heat to boiling point and then throw away water.
3. Repeat until fish tastes fresh and with just enough salt to taste.
4. Remove skin and bones (you can also buy already deboned salted cod fish) and break pieces of fish into even smaller pieces.
5. Mix fish with remaining ingredients. Serve with hard-boiled eggs, sliced avocado, and bakes.

FRENCH-SPEAKING

MARTINIQUE

In Martinique, breadfruit pudding is a popular dessert.

Breadfruit Pudding

1 pound breadfruit, peeled, cooked, and mashed	1 teaspoon grated lemon peel
½ cup sugar	2 cups light cream
¼ cup butter, melted	2 eggs, lightly beaten
1 tablespoon corn starch	1 teaspoon vanilla extract
	2 tablespoons dark rum

1. To prepare fresh breadfruit, peel and slice the fruit in half, remove the core, cube, and cook as you would potatoes, boiling for 15 to 20 minutes.
2. Combine all the ingredients in a bowl and beat until smooth.
3. Pour the batter into a well-buttered baking dish and bake in a preheated 350? F. oven for about 1½ hours, or until a tester comes out clean.
4. Serve warm with a cream sauce, a rum sauce, or ice cream.

HAITI

Griots is regarded as the finest and most popular Hatian dish.

Griots

2 pounds pork, cut in cubes	¼ cup water
1 cup chopped onions	* pinch of thyme
¼ cup chives, chopped	¼ teaspoon salt
½ cup lime juice	¼ teaspoon black pepper

1. Put all ingredients in bowl and allow to marinate a few hours. Drain.
2. Heat some oil, brown meat, then add marinade and simmer over low heat for 30 minutes, covered.
3. Remove lid and increase heat to remove any liquid. Serve hot.

GUADELOUPE

This is a popular dish in Guadeloupe, a country that adores seafood and cre-ole cuisine.

Accras de Morue

1 pound salted codfish, preferably deboned	1 egg
1½ cups all-purpose flour	1 garlic clove, minced
1 teaspoon baking powder	1 small fresh hot pepper, seeded and
1 cup milk	finely chopped

1. Soak the codfish in cold water for 2 hours (or bring the water to a rolling boil. Boil for 5 minutes to remove excess salt quickly).
2. Drain and then clean the codfish of any skin and bones. Flake or finely chop and set aside.
3. Sift the flour and baking powder into a medium-sized bowl.
4. Whisk together the milk and egg in another bowl, then combine with the flour mixture.
5. Combine all the seasoning ingredients and flaked codfish, and mix into a sticky batter. Taste and add salt and pepper, if necessary.
6. Heat the oil in a deep fryer or a large, heavy frying pan, then add the batter by the tablespoon.
7. Fry each side until golden brown, turning occasionally and pressing flat with a spatula. Serve hot as an appetizer, snack, or side dish.

DUTCH-SPEAKING

Aruba, Bonaire and Curacao are Dutch-speaking countries and are referred to as the ABC Islands. They make liberal use of soy sauce and satay in their cuisine.

ARUBA

Bolita di Keshi

1 pound Edam cheese, finely grated	5 tablespoons corn starch
6 eggs, well beaten	Vegetable oil for deep frying

1. Combine the cheese, eggs, and corn starch in a bowl and mix well.
2. Then shape into small balls, about 2 teaspoons to a ball.
3. Heat the vegetable oil, add the cheese balls, and fry until golden brown. Serve hot as an appetizer or party hors d' oeuvres on toothpicks.

BONAIRE

Keshi Yena Coe Galinja

3-pound to 4-pound Edam cheese	3 tomatoes, peeled, seeded, and chopped
2 pounds chicken, preferably breasts and thighs	1 large green pepper, seeded and chopped
1 onion, finely chopped	1 tablespoon fresh parsley leaves
* Salt and pepper	2 tablespoons tomato paste
1 teaspoon poultry seasoning	¼ cup sliced pimento stuffed olives
2 tablespoons butter	1 tablespoon capers
2 onions, sliced	¼ cup raisins
	2 tablespoons chopped gherkins

1. Strip the outer wax wrapping from the cheese and cut off about an inch from the top.
2. Scoop out the cheese, leaving a shell about 1 inch thick. Put the shell aside, and use the scooped-out cheese.
3. Rub the chicken pieces with the chopped onion, salt and pepper to taste, and poultry seasoning. Let stand for at least 2 hours at room temperature.
4. Arrange the chicken in a baking dish and broil until brown. Remove from the broiler and bake at 350°F. for 1 hour. Remove any skin and bones and shred the meat into fine pieces.
5. Heat the butter in a large skillet and add the sliced onions, tomatoes, green pepper, parsley, and hot pepper sauce.
6. Sauté for about 3 minutes, stirring regularly. Stir in the tomato paste, olives, capers, raisins, gherkins, and shredded chicken. Reduce the heat and simmer for about 20 minutes. Remove from the heat and cool.
7. Stuff the reserved cheese shell with the chicken mixture and top with the cheese lid. Place the filled shell in a large greased casserole.
8. Bake in a preheated 350°F. oven for about 30 minutes, or until the cheese becomes soft. Transfer to a serving dish and cut into wedges to serve.

Curacao

Fisherman's Soup

1 medium-size lobster, cooked,
    or ½ pound cooked lobster meat
¼ pound raw shrimp with shells
¼ pound white-fleshed fish fillet
6 cups chicken stock
1 onion, sliced
2 potatoes, peeled and sliced
   2 bay leaves, crumbled

2 garlic cloves
2 tablespoons tomato paste 2 large
    tomatoes, seeded and chopped
¼ cup cooking sherry
* Salt and freshly ground pepper
1 tablespoon butter

1. If the lobster and shrimp are in their shells, remove and chop the meat, reserving the shells.
2. Combine the fish fillet with the chicken stock in a large saucepan and poach until the fish flakes easily.
3. Remove the fish from the stock, chop, and set aside with the lobster and shrimp.
4. Add the reserved shells (if used) to the stock and cook over medium heat for 15 minutes, then remove and discard the shells.
5. Add all the ingredients, except the seafood and butter, to the stock and cook for another 15 minutes.
6. Remove the saucepan from the heat and blend the soup in batches in an electric blender or food processor.
7. Return the blended stock to heat, stir in the butter, and add the seafood. Cover and simmer for 5 minutes. Serve hot.

SPANISH-SPEAKING

The islands of the Spanish-speaking regions incorporate lots of cilantro and annatto in their cuisine.

CUBA

Cuban Chargrilled Lamb with Onions and Peppers

4 tablespoons finely chopped
    fresh flat-leaf parsley
1 tablespoon sweet paprika
4 cloves garlic, crushed
1 teaspoon salt
3 tablespoons olive oil
8 lamb loin chops

2 medium red onions, sliced thinly
2 medium green peppers,
    cut into 1 cm strips
1 medium yellow pepper,
    cut into 1 cm strips
2 tablespoons white wine

1. Blend or process parsley, paprika, garlic, salt and 1 tablespoon of the oil until mixture forms a paste. Spread paste over lamb until coated, cover; refrigerate 1 hour.
2. Heat remaining oil in large saucepan, add onion; cook until onion is soft. Add peppers; cook 2 minutes.
3. Add wine, cover; simmer gently, stirring occasionally, 20 minutes.
4. Meanwhile, cook lamb in grill pan (or on barbecue or under grill) until cooked through.
5. Serve lamb with onion and peppers, accompanied by mashed sweet potato and a green salad, if desired.

DOMINICAN REPUBLIC

Rice with Shrimp and Tomatoes

¼ cup chopped salt pork (2 ounces)
1 large onion, finely chopped
3 garlic cloves, minced
1 small fresh hot pepper, seeded and minced
4 cups chicken stock or 3 cups water
    and 1 cup chicken stock
2 cups rice

2 cups tomatoes, peeled, seeded,
    and chopped
* salt and freshly ground pepper
2 tablespoons butter
2 pounds raw shrimp, cleaned,
    deveined, and chopped
1 teaspoon dried parsley

1. Fry the salt pork until crisp in a large, heavy saucepan. Remove and drain on paper towels.
2. Add the onion, garlic, and hot pepper to the pork fat and sauté for about 2 minutes.
3. Pour in the chicken stock or water, then add the rice and tomatoes. Stir, then add salt and pepper to taste. Bring to a boil, reduce the heat, cover, and cook for about 25 minutes.
4. Heat the butter in a skillet, add the shrimp, and sauté for about 5 minutes.
5. When the rice is tender and the liquid is all absorbed, add the shrimp, salt pork, and parsley, mixing thoroughly. Cover and simmer for another 5 to 10 minutes. Serve hot.

PUERTO RICO

Paella

2 pounds raw chicken, cut into
    portion-sized pieces
1 pound raw red snapper fillet
    (or other white fish), cubed
1 pound raw lobster meat, chopped
1 pound raw shrimp, cleaned,
    deveined, and chopped
2 garlic cloves, minced
* salt
½ cup white wine
½ cup vegetable oil (olive oil is recommended)

1 bay leaf
2 tablespoons Sofrito
4 cups water
3 cups uncooked rice
4 chorizos (Spanish sausages),
    sliced diagonally
6 boiled chopped clams or 1(10-ounce)
    can Goya Red Clam Sauce
6 stuffed olives
1 fresh hot pepper, seeded and minced

1. Combine the chicken, red snapper, lobster, and shrimp in a large casserole. Season with the garlic and salt to taste, and add the white wine. Marinate for at least 2 hours (or overnight).
2. Heat ¼ cup of the oil in a very large saucepan. Remove the chicken pieces from the marinade, add to the saucepan, and sauté until all sides are evenly browned.
3. Add the bay leaf, Sofrito, and water to the saucepan; cover and bring to a boil.
4. Simmer for 10 minutes, taste for salt, and add the rice. Cover, return to medium heat, and cook for 15 minutes.
5. Heat the remaining ¼ cup oil in a skillet. Remove the fish, lobster, and shrimp from the marinade and add to the skillet.
6. Quickly sauté for 5 minutes. Reduce the heat and add the sausages, clams or clam sauce, olives, and hot pepper and sauté for 2 to 3 minutes.
7. Then combine the contents of the skillet with the chicken and rice, stirring well. Cover the saucepan and simmer for 5 minutes more.
8. Remove from the heat and serve hot with garlic bread, white wine, and a salad.

Menus

Brunch

Hot-buttered Rum or Carrot Punch*
Quickie Jerk Pork Snacks
Solomon Gundy
Banana Muffins
Bombay Mango Fool**

Boo Boo's Special*
Curried Codfish
Fruited Cabbage
Baps
Katie's Short bread
Coffee á la Mike*

Policeman Glow*
Ackee & Saltfish
Stuffed Breadfruit
Callaloo Salad
Matrimony**

Bloody Mary*
Escoveitch of Fish (Grouper)
Bammy
Naseberry Pancakes served with
syrup and butter, or orange jelly
Jamaican Coffee*

Coffee Coconut*
Crab Fritters
Cucumber and Sour Cream Salad
garnished with sweet peppers
Pumpkin Bread served with
tomato jam
Tropical Fruit Salad

Sour-Sop Punch*
Liver with sweet pepper
Cassava Puffs served with
pineapple jam
Ambrosia
Coffee á la Blue Mountain

Naked Lady* or
Hot Barbados Rum Egg Nog*
Fresh Fruit Plate
Pepper Shrimps
Ackee with Cheese
Jamaican Bun

Lunch

Hot Flashes*
Jamaica Fish Pie
Pumpkin Salad garnished with
sweet pepper rings and parsley
Otaheite Pudding

Pineapple Cocktail*
Jamaica Fish Tea
Broad Bean Salad
Beef & Mango in beer
Yam Casserole
Sliced Tomatoes
Orange Sorbet

Air Conditioner*
Pepperpot Soup
Chicken Salad
Sweet Pepper Salad
Pumpkin Bread
Coconut Mould

Banana Punch*
Coco Soup
Tropical Chicken
Stringbean Salad
Rum Coffee Jelly

Woodpecker*
Jamaican Salad
Curried Goat with rice
Mammee Apple Pie

Special Jamaican Rum Punch (hot)*
Fish Chowder
Poor Man's Fillet
Peas & Rice
Carrot and Raisin Salad
Guava Mousse

Spanish Town*
Pumpkin Soup
Marinated Pork Chops
Cho-cho Salad
Breadfruit Salad
Coconut Cream Pie

Dinner

Desperate Virgin*
Grapefruit with shrimp & sour cream
Jamaican Salad
Bahamian Conch Soup
Salmi of Duck
Pumpkin Puff
Cho-chos baked with cheese
Guava Layer Cake

Suffering Bastard*
or Starapple Appetizer
Avocado & Grapefruit Salad
Gungo Pea Soup
Pork Chops with Pineapple

Baked Sweet Potatoes
Guava Mousse

Clarendon Cocktail*
Ackee Salad
Red Pea Soup
Dumperpumpkin with rice
Onion Salad
Guava Pie

Frozen Daiquiri (Stella's Joy)*
Lobster Salad
Barbecued Lamb Chops
Callaloo Bake
Mint-Glazed Carrots
Orange Ice Box Dessert

Pineapple Caribbean*
Bahamian Conch Salad
Barbecued Chicken
Corn Fritters
Cauliflower Custard
Banana Pudding

Dry Martini*
Shrimp Salad with coconut cream
Cold Thick Cucumber Soup
Deboned Stuffed Leg of Kid with
browned potatoes
Egg Plant with Cheese & tomatoes
Carrot Ambrosia
Ripe Banana Pie

West Indian Punch*
Tropical Salad
Cho-cho Puree
King-Fish Fillets
Yam Casserole
Beans in sour cream sauce
Lime Pie

* See "Caribbean Cocktails" by Mike Henry   ** See "Jamaican Cocktails" by Mike Henry

GLOSSARY OF COOKING TERMS

BAIN MARIE — A French cooking utensil similar to a double boiler used to cook over boiling water

Bake — To cook by dry heat, usually in an oven

Barbecue — Generally refers to food cooked outdoors over an open fire with a spicy sauce

Baste — To brush or spoon liquid over food while cooking to keep it moist

Batter — Any combination that includes flour, milk, butter, eggs or the like, for pan-cakes, coating, dipping etc.

Beat — To mix with a whisk beater or spoon so as to make the mixture smooth

Blanch — To heat in boiling water or steam for a short period only to loosen skin, remove colour or set colour

Blend — To mix two or more ingredients thoroughly

Boil — To cook in any liquid at boiling point

CHILL — To place in refrigerator until cold

Coat — To cover entire surface of food with flour, bread-crumbs, or batter

Cream — To combine butter or other shortening with sugar using a wooden spoon or mixer until light and fluffy.

Croutons — Small cubes of fried bread

Cut in — To mix batter or margarine with dry ingredients, with a pastry blender, knives or fork

DEBONE — To remove bones from meat, poultry, game and fish

Deep Fry — To cook in deep, hot fat or oil, which covers the food until crisp and golden

Dice — To cut into small cubes

Disjoint — To separate the joints of poultry etc.

Dot — To scatter small bits of butter or margarine over surface of food

FLAME — To spoon alcoholic fluid over and ignite, to warm the alcohol, and pour flaming over food

Fold in — To use a spoon in a gentle rolling circular action as a means of combining ingredients

Fry — To cook in hot fat using moderate to high heat

GHEE — Clarified butter, used in curries

Glaze — A thin coating of beaten egg-milk, syrup or aspic which is brushed over pastry, fruits, ham, chicken etc.

Grate — To rub food against a grater to form small particles

Grill	To cook by direct heat either over a charcoal fire or under a gas or electric grill unit	SALMI	A hash, usually of duck
		Sauté	To fry lightly in a small amount of fat turning and stirring frequently
JULIENNE	A term for foods cut into thin strips like matches		
		Scald	To pour boiling water over foods, or bring to a boil
KNEAD	To work dough with hands until it is of the desired elasticity or consistency		
		Score	To cut narrow gashes on the surface of foods
MARINADE	Liquid used for seasoning by soaking usually a mixture of oil, wine and seasonings	Shred	To cut into fine strips
		Simmer	To cook in liquid just below boiling point
Marinate	To soak in a marinade to soften or add flavour		
		Skim	To remove foam, fat or solid substances from the surface of a cooking mixture
PARBOIL	To boil until partly cooked		
Pate	A highly seasoned meat paste		
		Sliver	To cut into long, thin strips
Pit	To remove pit-stone or seed from fruit	Steam	To cook in vapour rising from boiling water
Poach	To cook gently in simmering liquid	Stew	A long slow method of cooking in liquid in a covered pan, to tenderize tough meats
Pound	To reduce to small particles or a paste, using a pestle and mortar		
		Stir	To blend ingredients with a circular motion
Preheat	To turn over to a selected temperature 10 minutes before it is needed	Stock	A liquid containing the flavours, extracts and nutrients of bones, meat, fish or vegetables, in which they are cooked
Puree	To press through a fine sieve or put through a food blender to produce a smooth mixture		
		TOAST	To brown in a toaster or oven
REDUCE	To cook over a high heat, uncovered until it is reduced to desired consistency	Toss	To mix lightly, using a fork and a spoon, for salads chiefly
Roast	To cook meat by dry heat in the oven or on a spit	WHIP	To beat rapidly with hand or electric beater or wire whisk
Roux	A mixture of fat and flour cooked slowly, stirring frequently, used to thicken sauces, soups etc.		

35 USEFUL COOKING & HOUSEHOLD HINTS

1. $\frac{1}{3}$ to ½ teaspoon of dried herbs = 1 tablespoon fresh herbs.

2. Rub ½ lime on your hands or cutting board to remove onion, garlic or fish odours.

3. To avoid trouble with weevils, keep flour or cornmeal in a glass jar or plastic container in the refrigerator.

4. 1 tablespoon oil in water for boiling pastas (macaroni etc.) prevents it from sticking together.

5. 1 lb. coffee brews 40 cups.

6. For a tender pie crust, use less water than is called for.

7. Dip knife in hot water to slice hard-boiled eggs.

8. 1 cup macaroni makes 2 cups of cooked macaroni.

9. Freeze left-over coffee in an ice cube tray. When used to chill iced coffee, the cubes will not dilute the coffee.

10. Parsley rinsed in hot water instead of cold retains more flavour.

11. Brown sugar will not become lumpy if stored in a jar with a piece of blotting paper fitted to the inside of the jar lid.

12. If food boils over in the oven, cover with salt to prevent smoking and excessive odour.

13. Add diced crisp bacon and a dash of nutmeg to cauliflower (or cabbage) for a gourmet touch.

14. To keep kettles clean, fill with cold water, add some ammonia and bring to a boil. Rinse well.

15. Gas ovens must be wiped clean before oven is cold. Racks and shelves must be washed with hot water and washing soda.

16. Wash pewter with hot water and soap, as polish will scratch the surface.

17. Mildew stains can be removed by soaking overnight in sour milk. Dry in the sun without rinsing. Repeat process if necessary.

18. To remove a scorch, spread a paste of starch and cold water over the mark. Dry in sun and brush off.

19. Wash glass windows with crumpled newspaper dipped in cold water, to which a few drops of ammonia has been added.

20. To get rid of wood worms, apply kerosene oil with a brush to the infected area daily for 10 days.

21. To stop doors from creaking, rub hinges with soap.

22. Rust marks can be removed from steel by rubbing with a cut onion.

23. When washing thermos flasks, add a little vinegar to the water. It removes the musty smell. Do not cork flasks when storing.

24. To remove stains from china, use a rag dipped in cold water and salt.

25. Before baking, ensure ingredients are at room temperature.

26. To chop sticky dried fruits, heat knife before using.

27. To prepare nuts, first blanch. Cover with cold water and bring to a boil. Let soak until they wrinkle, then slip the skin off between the fingers.

28. Parsley freezes well. Cut stems and place them in a plastic bag. Thaws easily as well.

29. Tear lettuce into pieces, instead of cutting, to prevent browning.

30. It is a good idea to make stock from left-over bones and keep in the freezer to enhance soups and sauces.

31. Soak tarnished silver in hot water and ammonia - 1 tablespoon ammonia to 1 quart water.

32. Sour milk can be made by adding two teaspoons of lime juice to a cup of warm milk, which will curdle.

33. Moulds should be oiled before they are filled. Custards baked in hot water should be removed and left to stand for 5 minutes to settle before unmoulding. Run knife around the edge. Place a plate over the mould, invert the plate and mould and lift off.

34. As soon as vegetables are tender, drain and plunge into cold water. This sets the colour. Vegetables may be stored and reheated when needed.

35. Whip cream in a large bowl set in ice. If no cream is available, place a tin of evaporated milk in the freezer for about one hour and then proceed to whip as for cream. To sweeten, use icing sugar, which is preferred to granulated sugar.

TABLE OF MEASUREMENTS AND MISCELLANEOUS EQUIVALENTS

Dash	=	Less than 1/8 teaspoon		
3 teaspoon	=	Tablespoon	=	15 ml
4 tablespoons	=	¼ cup	=	60 ml
8 tablespoons	=	½ cup	=	120ml
16 tablespoons	=	1 cup	=	240 ml
1 cup	=	½ pint	=	240 ml
2 cups	=	1 pint	=	480 ml
4 cups	=	1 quart	=	960 ml or .95 litres
2 liquid cups	=	1 lb.		
2 pints	=	1 quart	=	960 ml or .95 litres
4 quarts	=	1 gallon	=	3.8 litres
1 fluid ounce	=	2 tablespoons	=	30 ml
8 fluid ounces	=	1 cup	=	240 ml
16 ounces	=	1 pound	=	480 ml
1 lb. butter	=	2 cups	=	454 grams
1 carrot	=	½ cup chopped		
¼ lb. cheese	=	1 cup grated		
1 envelope gelatin	=	1 tablespoon		
1 teaspoon dried herbs	=	1 tablespoon		
Fresh juice of 1 lime	=	1 tablespoon		
1 medium onion	=	¾ cup chopped		
1 medium potato	=	¼ cup chopped		
1 pack dry yeast	=	¾ oz.	=	21 grams

SOME SUBSTITUTIONS

When you do not have exactly what the recipe calls for, here are some suggestions for acceptable substitutes.

1 square cooking chocolate	=	3 tablespoons cocoa + 1 oz. butter
1 cup self-raising flour	=	1 cup plain flour + 2 teaspoons of baking powder
1 cup sour milk	=	1 tablespoon lime juice or white vinegar + 1 cup milk
1 cup fresh milk	=	½ cup evaporated milk + ½ cup water
1 cup sour cream	=	1 cup warm milk + 1 tablespoon lime juice or white vinegar. Stirred to a thick consistency.
Yeast compressed (1 oz.)	=	2 teaspoons active dry yeast
1 fresh garlic clove	=	¼ teaspoon garlic powder
fresh green root ginger, grated	=	¼-½ teaspoon ground ginger

MEAL TIME: QUANTITIES PER HEAD

Appetizers	a variety of 4 - 6
Soup	5 servings to 1 quart
Sauces	10 servings to 1 pint
Fish	6 ozs. without bone, 8 ozs. with bone
Meat	4 ozs. without bone, 6 ozs. with bone
Green vegetables	6 servings 8 ozs
Potatoes	4 servings 8 ozs
Puddings/cold sweets	3 servings to 1 pint
Ices	10 servings to 1 quart
Poultry (chicken)	6 portions from a 4 lb. chicken
Poussin (chicken 3 - 4 weeks old)	1 portion

USEFUL KITCHEN EQUIPMENT

Cake tester	Blender
Poultry shears	Food chopper
Colander	Meat pounder
Rotary egg whisk	Nut grinder
Pastry blender	Pots, pans, casseroles
Pastry brush	Knives
Cheese graters	Sieves, rubber scrapers, bulb basters

Pots must be heavy-bottomed. The best all-purpose material is undoubtedly heavy-enamelled cast iron. Copper pots are very satisfactory - the metal should be 1/8" thick and the handle should be made of iron. A kitchen should have round and oval casseroles. Saucepans of various sizes - a skillet (sloping sides) and a sauté pan (straight sides).

Omelette Pan - This can be made of iron, with a long handle and a 2" sloping side and a 7" diameter bottom. This is perfect for 2 - 3 egg omelettes. When new, scrub with steel wool and scouring powder. Rinse and dry. Heat it and rub bottom with oil and let it stand overnight. Just before using, sprinkle 1 teaspoon of salt in the pan and rub with a paper towel.

Knives must be of good quality, and kept in good condition: a 9" blade for chopping vegetables, a pointed knife for filleting, which should have a 6½" flexible blade. Knives for splitting chickens should have a 12" blade and should be heavy.
A carver should only be used for carving.

INDEX